THE ACTS OF ANDREW

Dennis R. MacDonald

POLEBRIDGE PRESS

Library of Congress Cataloging-in-Publication Data

Acts of Andrew. English.
  Acts of Andrew/[translated by] Dennis MacDonald.
     p. cm.
  Includes bibliographical references (p.) and indexes.
  ISBN 0-944344-55-0
  I. MacDonald, Dennis Ronald, 1946- II. Title.

BS2880.A37A3 2005
229'.925--dc22

2005048657

CONTENTS

SERIES PREFACE

The series *Early Christian Apocrypha & (ECA&)*, the first such publication by north American scholars, is designed as a study edition of early Christian apocryphal texts and related writings. These comprise the standard set of New Testament apocrypha (gospels, acts, epistles, apocalypses) along with other, some less well known, writings that emerged from the early Christian movement, such as homiletical, polemical, exegetical, and church order tracts. Writings reckoned "orthodox" and "heretical" by contemporaries and later authorities will be included.

The publisher and the editors have had several goals in mind. First, to provide quotable and lively renderings into modern U.S. English—satisfying both to the specialist and to the non-expert reader. Second, to offer full introductions and bibliographies that will situate the texts in question in their larger Christian and Greco-Roman contexts. Third, to supply brief commentary explaining technical aspects of the writing and the movement of the text.—storyline or theological argument. Fourth, to add "verse numbers" where previous editions gave only larger section or chapter numbers.

Where appropriate, the texts will be annotated with cross-references, not only within the biblical canon but also outside it—in due course supplying a network of interconnected references to assist comparative study. A full index of texts, biblical and non-biblical, will conclude each volume.

SIGLA

A	The Anglo-Saxon epic poem *Andreas*
AA	*Ann Arbor gr. 36*, ms of the Greek Passion
AAM	The *Acts of Andrew and Matthias*
Arm	The Armenian version of the Passion
AS	The Anglo-Saxon version of the *AAM*
B	*Bologna 1576*, an eleventh-century Latin ms of the *AAM*
BC	Bodleian Coptic manuscript
C	*Recensio Casanatensis*, a Latin version of the *AAM*
Cd	A Latin version of the Passion
E	The ninth-century *Life of Andrew* by Epiphanius
Ep	*L'Épître grecque*, a Latin version of the Passion
Eth	The Ethiopic version of the *AAM*
GE	The Latin *Epitome* by Gregory of Tours
Gr	The Greek mss used by Bonnet for the *AAM*
Grm	Many of the Greek mss for the *AAM*
Grp	Few of the Greek mss for the *AAM*
HS	*Jerusalem, St. Sabas 103* and *Sinai gr 526* (BG 94h), The Greek Passion
L	The ninth-century *Laudatio* of Andrew by Nicetas the Paphlagonian
Lat	The Latin and Anglo-Saxon versions of the *AAM*
LSJ	Liddell Scott Jones
M	The Greek *Martyrium prius*, of the late eighth century
Ma	The Greek *Martyrium alterum*, witnessed from eleventh and fourteenth centuries
N	The *Narratio* of the late eighth century
O	*Ottoban 415*, Greek ms of the *AAM*
P	The Greek ms *Parisinus gr. 1313*
Pas	Passion of Andrew
PCU	*Papyrus Coptic Utrecht*
P.Oxy. 851	*Papyrus Oxyrhynchus 815*, a Greek fragment of the *AAM*
Syr	The Syriac version of the *AAM*
V	*Recension Vaticana 1274*, a Latin version of the *AAM*
Vat	*Vaticanus graecus 808*, a tenth- or eleventh-century Greek fragment of the Passion

INTRODUCTION

The *Acts of Andrew* is one of numerous examples of early Christian narratives that relate the adventures and mission of the apostles and disciples of Jesus after the resurrection. *Andrew* is numbered among the five "major" acts, the others being the *Acts of Paul*, the *Acts of Peter*, the *Acts of John*, and the *Acts of Thomas*. Each document presents its own special problems of translation and interpretation, though all five present such difficulties as assessing the original length of the work and the correct ordering of its episodes; collating the various recensions in several languages; retrieving quotations from patristic and medieval authors; and identifying multiple layers of editing in the course of transmission. Also of crucial importance is to discover how these works were either appropriated by "unorthodox" groups and hence discredited along with other apocryphal writings, or were made theologically more acceptable to a later generation through a process of "catholicizing" redaction that often included extensive omission of supposedly offensive material.

THE ACTS OF ANDREW
Transmission and Survival

The *Acts of Andrew* now exists only in fragments, epitomes, and derivative recensions. Some sections are gone forever; much of the content is represented only by a tendentious and frequently garbled sixth-century Latin epitome by Gregory of Tours (ca. 540–594), a critical edition of which was published by Maximillian Bonnet in 1885 (see bibliography). In 1911, Josef Flamion issued a penetrating study of these textual remains, though he did not himself prepare an edition based on his findings. Unavailable to Flamion were several witnesses that have recently come to light, most notably more reliable and extensive versions of the martyrdom of Andrew.

Flamion's research, and especially these new texts, allow for a tolerably reliable reconstruction of the *Acts of Andrew*. Recently, Jean-Marc Prieur and Dennis Ronald MacDonald have independently reassembled from these sundry pieces much of the *Acts*. The translation that follows is based on the MacDonald edition, though that of Prieur must of course be consulted by the serious student.

Even though these editions largely agree, they differ greatly with respect to the role of the separately transmitted *Acts of Andrew and Matthias* in the construction of the *Acts of Andrew*. MacDonald claims that some version of *Andrew and Matthias* once appeared at the beginning of *Andrew*; Prieur, concurring with the judgment of Flamion, claims that it was written much later. (It should be noted that several other clearly later texts feature Andrew along with fellow apostles, among them the *Acts of Peter and Andrew*, the *Acts of Andrew and Paul*.) Extended arguments for and against including the *Acts of Andrew and Matthias* are set out in the introduction to MacDonald's edition, and a brief discussion of the matter is also in order here.

THE ACTS OF ANDREW AND MATTHIAS

The *Acts of Andrew and Matthias* begins with the apostles in Jerusalem casting lots to see where each will preach. It falls to Matthias to evangelize "the city of the cannibals," which Gregory and Latin witnesses name Myrmidonia. When the apostle arrives in that city, the residents gouge out his eyes and imprison him for thirty days of fattening. Jesus appears to Andrew, who is preaching in Achaea, and tells him to go to Myrmidonia to rescue his fellow apostle. Proceeding to the seacoast, Andrew finds a boat going to the cannibal land, but fails to notice that Jesus himself is the captain and two angels constitute his crew.

Upon reaching his destination, Andrew goes to the prison, slays the guards with a prayer, and rescues Matthias and the other prisoners. Discovering that the apostle has set free their anticipated food supply, the residents seize him, drag him through the streets for three days, and leave him for dead. Jesus revives him, however, whereupon he commands a statue to spew forth a flood, thereby drowning many of the city's inhabitants. The only survivors are those who repent with tears and ashes. Andrew orders the flood to cease, and an abyss swallows the waters along with the would-be executioners and a merciless old man. The apostle raises the dead—both humans and beasts—and promises to return to rescue those consumed by the abyss, but only after they have observed in the world below the tortures of the wicked and the rewards of the righteous. Andrew then leaves town, in spite of being urged by the cannibals to remain. As the apostle sails away, Jesus appears to him and rebukes him for his callous disregard of the people's entreaties. Andrew returns to the city and teaches for seven days, but fails to retrieve anyone from the abyss. Throughout, the account shows unmistakable dependence on the Septuagint version of the book of Jonah.

A much abbreviated form of this narrative begins the epitome by Gregory of Tours, but in that story the apostle continues his adventures through Anatolia, Thrace, Macedonia, and back to Achaea, where he is executed in Patras. In other words, Gregory's account contains a circular itinerary that is unique among the early apocryphal acts, the extant remains of which typically show the apostles proceeding on a one-way journey from Jerusalem to the region of their appointed ministries and death.

Flamion concluded that this unusual itinerary and the obvious stylistic differences between the cannibal story and the rest of the *Acts* demonstrate that the Frankish bishop actually epitomized not one book, but two: the *Acts of Andrew and Matthias in the City of the Cannibals* and the *Acts of Andrew*. In his view, Gregory's less than adept suturing fails to conceal the original gap between them (Flamion: 269–324). Not all scholars have followed Flamion's opinion, however. Richard Adelbert Lipsius's dissent (Lipsius, 1883–90: 1. 546–53, 601, 615) was followed, for example, by Otto Bardenhewer, Adolf Harnack, Albert Ehrhard, and M. Blumenthal.

Flamion further argued that Gregory's naming of the city of the cannibals "Myrmidonia" shows that he knew only a derivative version of the story, inasmuch as the city was unnamed in the original. To be sure, the best Greek texts of the *Acts of Andrew and Matthias* do not contain the word Myrmidonia, but it now appears that the original story, like Gregory's epitome, did. Nineteen years after Flamion's study, Franz Blatt published the first edition of the *Recensio Casanatensis*, a reasonably faithful Latin translation of the *Acts of Andrew and Matthias* dating to the sixth or seventh century, and thus at least a century earlier than the surviving Greek witnesses; in it we find several references to Myrmidonia.

In fact, all extant texts in Latin or Anglo-Saxon contain some reference to this city by name, even though many of their copyists were unsure how to spell it. The manuscripts of the epitome by Gregory of Tours variously read Mermidona, Mirmidona, Mirmidonia, Mirmydona, Myrmidona, and Myrmidonia (here listed alphabetically; see Bonnet, 1885: 827). To make matters even more confusing, other related western documents read Myrmidon, Myrmidonensis, Mermedonia, Marmedonia, and Marmadonia (see Brooks: xxix; Krapp: lxvi; Blatt: 6–7, 141). We also find Medea (in an eighth-century manuscript of the *Martyrdom of Matthew*, see Lipsius-Bonnet: 2/1. 218), as well as Margundia (see Voragine, *Legenda aurea:* 13) and Mirdone (in the Old French *Vie saint Andrier l'apostle*, see Baker: 439). Furthermore, it would be wrong to conclude that the name was known only in western Christendom. Greek texts undoubtedly related to the *Acts of Andrew and Matthias* give the city name as Μυρμήνη (in an eleventh-century manuscript of the *Martyrdom of Andrew*, see Lipsius-Bonnet: 2/1. 220 and also in Nicephorus Callistus, *Ecclesiastical Histories* 2.41); Μυρμήνις (in a ninth-century manuscript of the *Martyrdom of Andrew*, Lipsius-Bonnet: 2/1. 47), Μύρνη (most manuscripts of the *Martyrdom*, Lipsius-Bonnet: 2/1. 2/1. 220); Μυρμήκη or Σμυρμήκη (*Paris gr. 1313*, unpublished); and Σμύρνα (a tenth-century manuscript of the *Martyrdom* (Lipsius-Bonnet: 2/1. 227, 262).

Just as baffling as its spelling but even more important for determining its function in the *Acts of Andrew and Matthias* is the city's location. Various suggestions have included Sinope, Athens, Titaran (unknown), Sebastopolis Magna (Greek "Colchis"), and, most popularly, Myrmekion, an ancient city on what is now the Crimean peninsula and in antiquity frequently related to

Scythia (Gutschmid: 161–83, 380–401). According to Eusebius (*Hist. eccl.* 3.1), Origen also placed Andrew's ministry in Scythia, and *Recensio Vaticana* (a seventh- or eighth-century Latin poem about Andrew, Matthias, and cannibals) places "Myrmidonia" (once identified as "Myrmidonensis") in Scythia. In light of the ancient stereotype of Scythians as cannibals (e.g., in Herodotus 4.18, 26; Aristotle, *Politica* 8.3.4; Strabo 11.2.12; Aeschylus, *Prometheus* 707–13; Tertullian, *Adv. Marc.* 1.1), this identification seems quite plausible and has enjoyed nearly unanimous acceptance.

There is good reason to judge, however, that this longstanding consensus is wrong. Myrmidonia belongs not on the map of the Roman Empire but on the map of the imagination; its significance is not geographical but mythological. In Myrmidonia live Myrmidons, who as early as Homer appear in Greek literature as allies of Achilles, and whose name, according to later mythology, derived from the Greek word for ant: μύρμηξ, plur. μύρμηκες. That is, they had once been ants, and although Zeus had made them human, they continued to behave like ants. For some interpreters, their formic traits were positive: they were industrious, thrifty, and courageous. But others took them to be "the most warlike of races" (see Lucian, *Icaromenippus* 19).

This latter interpretation seems to underlie the *Acts of Andrew and Matthias*. Threads of Myrmidonian ancestry are woven so deeply into the fabric of the story that even the Greek manuscripts lacking the word "Myrmidonia" depict the city as "Antville." In order to bake their victims, the cannibals have erected at the center of the city a huge oven (κλίβανος). In antiquity, one built an oven by digging several feet down into the earth and forming mud and plaster into conical walls with an opening at the top. In other words, the large κλίβανος would have looked very much like an anthill. Their social organization also suggests that of ants: they have no king, no proconsul, no magistrate, only "rulers" (ἄρχοντες), "superiors" (μείζονες), "guards" (φύλακες), "executioners" (δήμιοι), and "the young," who sail away in search of prey. Just as some ants bite their victims, poisoning them into submission, so the cannibals drug their victims into beastlike domestication. They repeatedly drag Andrew through their streets, like ants hauling their quarry to the nest. Indeed, by way of punishment Andrew tries to drown them—a common means of exterminating ants. When the residents repent, Andrew calls off the flood, walks toward the middle of town, and the waters recede before him until he gets to the vat and the oven. There the earth opens and the abyss swallows the waters along with the most wicked of the cannibals—like ants plunged into their underground chambers.

It would therefore appear that the textual ancestor behind most extant Greek versions of the *Acts* tendentiously removed every trace of Μυρμιδονία, presumably because of its fabulous antecedents in Greek myth. Latin and Anglo-Saxon manuscripts, however, retained the name—in thirteen different spellings!—because western readers, for whom ants were *formicae* or *aemettes*, were unaware of the disreputable ancestry of Myrmidonia as the city of μύρμηκες.

This reading of the evidence further suggests that by detaching the Myrmidon story from the *Acts of Andrew*, Flamion turned one literary mess into two. Without the Myrmidon story at its beginning, the *Acts of Andrew* begins in landlocked Amasia, without any indication concerning how or why the apostle went there. Most glaring is the narrative hiatus in the *Acts of Andrew and Matthias* when the additional plot elements are omitted. The text is explicit about what should occur: Andrew is to leave the city and rejoin the disciples (chap. 32), go with them to "the city of the barbarians" (chap. 33), and return to Myrmidonia to raise the fifteen swallowed by the abyss (chap. 31). Andrew never does any of this. Rather than presenting any kind of denouement, the story ends prematurely with Andrew sailing off to find his disciples.

This unresolved ending clearly bothered ancient readers, as one can see from the attempts either to expunge from the text these promises never kept or to supply the foreshadowed but wanting episodes (see MacDonald, 1990: 17–18). Such early readers were surely right: the story is obviously incomplete. Even though Gregory's epitome does not actually narrate the episodes anticipated at the end of the *Acts of Andrew and Matthias*, it does provide a legitimate beginning to the *Acts of Andrew* and a plausible transition from Myrmidonia to Amasia.

In addition to these factors, we find the following external witnesses weighing heavily in favor of including the Myrmidon story at the beginning of the *Acts of Andrew*: *Pseudo-Epiphanius*, *Pseudo-Hippolytus*, the fourth-century Syriac *Doctrina apostolorum*, Basil of Seleucia (d. ca. 439), Nicetas the Paphlagonian, Theophanes Cerameus, Nicephorus Callistus Xanthopoulus, and the great Byzantine "librarian" Photius (ca. 810–ca. 895) (full details in MacDonald, 1990: 19–27). Unfortunately, these witnesses derive from the fifth to the thirteenth centuries, when hagiographic devotion may have conflated traditions ultimately derived from different sources, or even artificially merged two originally discrete *Acts* into a single volume. It is possible, however, to push the inquiry back as far as the early third century by demonstrating that other apocryphal acts apparently dependent on the *Acts of Andrew* knew not only undisputed section of the *Acts of Andrew* but the Myrmidon story as well. This is the case with the *Acts of Thomas*, the *Acts of Philip*, the *Acts of John* by Prochorus, and probably the *Acts of Xanthippe and Polyxena* (MacDonald, 1990: 27–45).

The manuscript legacy of the *Acts of Andrew* itself bears traces of the primitive attachment of the Myrmidon story. The *Martyrium prius* (late eighth century; in Lipsius-Bonnet: 2/1. 46–57), whose author, like Gregory, seems to have had access to the entire *Acts of Andrew* (though probably in a derivative recension), likewise begins with the apostolic lottery in Jerusalem. Andrew

draws Bithynia, Sparta, and Achaea. In addition, Matthew (frequently con-
fused with Matthias) is assigned to τὴν Μυρμηνίδα πόλιν, "the city Myrmenis," undoubtedly a variant of Μυρμιδονία. Three Byzantine documents
narrate Andrew's adventures on the way from Jerusalem to Patras, and each
alludes to the Myrmidon story: these are the *Life of Andrew*, written by a
ninth-century monk named Epiphanius; a panegyric conventionally entitled
the *Laudatio*, largely dependent on Epiphanius and written by the already
mentioned Nicetas the Paphlagonian; and an eighth- or ninth-century passion of Andrew known as the *Narratio*. Gregory, Epiphanius, *Laudatio*, and
Narratio seldom agree, but they do on this basic narrative scheme: Andrew is
sent out from Jerusalem, he quickly finds himself in the region of the Black
Sea, he rescues Matthias from savages (his first fully narrated act), and after
other exploits travels to Achaea, where he dies on a cross (Gregory, *Epitome* 1;
Epiphanius, *Panarion* 217D–224A; *Laudatio* 7–8; *Narratio* 5–7).

AUTHORSHIP

Innocent I (early fifth century), in a letter to Exsuperius of Toulouse, lists
books condemned by the church, including the *Acts of Andrew*. He claims that
this *Acts* was the work of "the philosophers Xenocharides and Leonidas"
(*vel sub nomine Andreae, quae a Xenocharide et Leonida philosophis* [PL 20.502]).
Surely this attribution of the *Acts* to two philosophers had already been made
prior to Innocent, who would have preferred labeling the authors heretics
rather than philosophers. Innocent is not the first to have attributed the *Acts
of Andrew* to more than one author. Philaster of Brescia (prior to 385), who
seems to have had access to the *Acts*, attributes the work to "disciples who
followed the apostles," whence, says Philaster, it fell into the hands of Manichaeans (PL 12.1200).

There are two possible explanations for the origin of these ascriptions to
multiple authors: (1) the names are later, artificial attributions, or (2) these
two philosophers actually wrote the work.

It is unlikely that the names are later attributions, for nothing apparent
was to be gained by attributing the work to characters otherwise unknown
in the *Acts* itself or in the early church. It would therefore appear more reasonable to think that Xenocharides and Leonidas actually wrote the *Acts of
Andrew*. This would match perfectly the statement by Innocent I, conform
with Philaster's assertion of multiple authorship, and explain the presence
of names inexplicable as pseudonyms. There can, in fact, be little doubt that
the *Passio* emerged from the pen of a sophisticated Christian Platonist, that
is, from a philosopher.

On the other hand, the three most reliable witnesses to the *Passio* all
conclude with a postscript written in the first person *singular*, beginning as
follows: "Hereabouts I should make an end of the blessed tales (διηγμάτων),

acts, and mysteries difficult —I should say impossible—to express. Let this stroke of the pen end it. I will pray first for myself, that I heard what was actually said (ἀκοῦσαι τῶν εἰρημένων ὡς εἴρηται)." That this statement is not merely a scribal colophon is clear from the author's conscious decision to terminate the narrative here. Its lexical and stylistic agreements with the *Acts of Andrew* likewise commend it as the work of the author.

Here is what may have happened. Originally, the *Acts of Andrew* began with Xenocharides and Leonidas introducing themselves, just as "Leucius" apparently did at the beginning of the *Acts of John* or as "the presbyters and deacons at the churches of Achaea" do at the beginning of a Latin Andrean passion account derived from the *Acts of Andrew*. The *Acts of Thomas* likewise begins in the first person plural: "At that time all of us, the apostles, were in Jerusalem." Prochorus, the fictitious author of the *Acts of John by Prochorus*, identifies himself at the conclusion of the apostolic lottery that begins the work.

Presumably the text identified Xenocharides and Leonidas as philosophers, one as an eyewitness, the other as the author. This would explain why the author of the postscript does not claim to have seen what happened but to have "heard what was said," that is, to have received reports from intermediary witnesses. This corresponds with statements from authors in the second century that they had heard about the apostles from their followers. Papias: "Whenever anyone came who had followed the ancients (πρεσβυτέροις), I inquired concerning the words of the ancients, what Andrew or Peter or Philip or Thomas or James or John or Matthew, or any other of the Lord's disciples, had said" (Eusebius, *Hist. eccl.* 3.39.4). "Ancients" or "presbyters" in this context seems to refer to people old enough to have heard the apostles in person. Irenaeus boasts that he had heard the preaching of Polycarp, who in turn had been "instructed by apostles" (*Adv. haer.* 3.3.4).

The names Xenocharides and Leonidas still appeared in the copy of the *Acts of Andrew* known to Innocent I (perhaps in a Latin translation), and probably in the copy known to Philaster, who mistook them for Andrew's disciples. The names disappeared from Gregory's epitome and from the Myrmidon story when it was detached from the rest of the *Acts*. The authorial postscript also dropped out of most versions of the *Passio*.

This reconstruction must of course remain hypothetical; the evidence precludes firm conclusions.

DATE AND PLACE OF COMPOSITION

Flamion judges that the *Acts of Andrew* was the product of an anonymous Christian intellectual in Patras, Achaea, who cherished a legend concerning the apostle's visit there (Flamion: 264–68). Achaea, however, is the one place in the Greek-speaking *oikoumene* almost certainly *not* the place of origin. No resident of Achaea would have supplied Patras, instead of Corinth, with a proconsul and a praetorium. Moreover, apart from the *Acts of Andrew* itself, no existing evidence places a Christian community in Patras until later.

Flamion seems also to have erred in dating the *Acts* to the second half of the third century on the basis of its similarities with Neoplatonism. This date is too late if the *Acts of Andrew* influenced the author of the *Acts of Thomas*. The Platonic commitments identified by Flamion correlate not only with Neoplatonism but with Middle Platonism as well.

Help in establishing the date and location of composition may come from a controverted passage in Eusebius:

> Thomas, as tradition (παράδοσις) relates, obtained by lot Parthia, Andrew Scythia, John Asia (and he stayed there and died in Ephesus), but Peter seems to have preached to the Jews of the Dispersion in Pontus and Galatia and Bithynia, Cappadocia, and Asia, and at the end he came to Rome and was crucified head downwards, for so he had demanded to suffer. What need be said of Paul, who fulfilled the gospel of Christ from Jerusalem to Illyria and afterward was martyred in Rome under Nero? This is stated exactly by Origen in the third volume of his commentary on Genesis. (*Hist. eccl.* [Loeb])

Eric Junod has shown, contra Harnack, that Eusebius did indeed receive this information from Origen's commentary, which had been written in Alexandria prior to his flight to Caesarea in 231 (Junod, 1981). Junod also suggests that Origen's listing of the very five apostles featured in the earliest of the apocryphal acts can hardly be coincidental, especially since Origen mentions John's death in Ephesus, Peter's inverted crucifixion, and Paul's execution by Nero—all episodes narrated in the apocryphal acts of those apostles. Surely Origen's παράδοσις somehow relates to the production of apocryphal acts. But how?

Because the references to Thomas in Parthia and Andrew in Scythia do not correspond precisely with the *Acts* of these apostles, Junod held back from claiming that Origen's information issued directly from the apocryphal acts. Albrecht Dihle has shown, however, that Origen's statement about Thomas in Parthia need not contradict the *Acts of Thomas* inasmuch as Parthian overlords at the time ruled much of northern India (Dihle). Furthermore, the version of the *Acts of Andrew* Junod had in mind had no Myrmidons, whose savagery so frequently identified them with Scythia (so the Latin *Recensio Vaticana*; the Anglo-Saxon poem *Andreas*; Epiphanius the monk; Nicephorus Callistus; *Pseudo-Epiphanius*; and *Pseudo-Hippolytus*). Had Origen himself read the *Acts of Andrew*, one can appreciate why he might have substituted historical Scythia for a Mymidonian never-never land.

Indeed, Origen's very wording suggests that his tradition derived from the apocryphal acts. Thomas, Andrew, and John are grouped together, each as a subject of the verb εἴληχεν, "obtained by lot." The verbs change with respect to Peter and Paul. They are not included in a lottery. Thomas's *Acts* begins with the casting of lots; he draws India. Andrew's *Acts*, if we include the Myrmidons, also begins with a lottery; Andrew draws Achaea and Matthias Myrmidonia. The beginning of the *Acts of John* is lost, but it too could well have begun with such a scene. If it did, he would have drawn Asia, where the apostle ministers in the rest of the *Acts of John*. It is striking that the three apostles whose acts either did or might have begun with a casting of lots are the same three that Origen makes the subject of the verb εἴληχεν.

It is therefore arguable that Origen's information about Andrew in Scythia and Thomas in Parthia, like his information about John in Ephesus, Peter upside down, and Paul beheaded, derived from apocryphal acts. If this is the case, an intellectual of the Great Church already considered the content of these acts established tradition by 231, and therefore the *Acts of Andrew* should probably be dated no later than 200, inasmuch as it influenced the composition of the *Acts of Thomas*. This is also the latest possible date for the *Acts of John*, with which the *Acts of Andrew* shares philosophical commitments, rhetorical patterns, and many literary motifs. Finally, Origen's apparent knowledge of the *Acts of Andrew*—with its distinctive version of Middle Platonism and its similarities to the *Acts of John*—points to Alexandria as the most likely place of composition.

CONTENT AND LITERARY DESIGN

The translation of the *Acts of Andrew* given below presents the literary remains in three Parts, to which are added three Miscellaneous Traditions. Part I is the *Acts of Andrew and Matthias in the City of the Cannibals*, and is based on a comparison of two independent yet widely attested text-types, distinguished from each other by language and geography. The first consists of the Greek manuscripts (nine of them, from the tenth to the sixteenth centuries) that Bonnet used to create his eclectic text (Lipsius-Bonnet: 2/1. 65–116) as well as translations into Syriac, Ethiopic, Coptic, and several Slavonic languages. Readings from this eastern text-type are identified with the siglum Gr (= Graeci, "Greek"), which generally corresponds with Bonnet's edition. Grm (=Graeci multi) indicates that a reading so designated is attested by many of these manuscripts; Grp (= Graeci pauci) indicates a reading that is attested by few.

The second text-type consists of all Latin and Anglo-Saxon translations and is designated with the siglum Lat (= Latini). These western manuscripts include the *Recensio Casanatensis* (= C, an abbreviated Latin version from the sixth or seventh century; Blatt: 32–95), *Codex Vallicellanus* (a Latin fragment of chaps. 17–18; Lipsius-Bonnet: 2/1. 85–88), *Bologna 1576* (= B, an abbreviated Latin recension; Baumler: 90–112), *Recensio Vaticana* (= V, a poetic Latin recension; Blatt: 96–148), and the Anglo-Saxon recensions (= AS): *Cambridge 198* (from the late tenth century; Goodwin: 2–15), *Blickling Homily XIX* (also from the tenth century; Morris: 2. 228–49), and the epic poem *Andreas* (= *A*; Krapp: 1–68).

These two major text-types, Gr and Lat, also differ with respect to the curious name of the cannibals' city. Every Latin and Anglo-Saxon version of the *Acts of Andrew and Matthias* (i.e., Gregory and the representatives of Lat) contains some form of the name Myrmidonia. Every manuscript represented by Gr, however, lacks it.

The single Greek manuscript of the *Acts of Andrew and Matthias* that contains references to Myrmidonia, *Paris gr 1313* (= *P*, fifteenth century), was known to Bonnet but ignored in his critical edition. It may represent an independent channel of textual transmission and supply bridges between the *Acts of Andrew and Matthias* and the rest of the *Acts of Andrew*. *P* once names the cannibals' city Σμυρμήνη and twice Μυρμήκη. Furthermore, unlike Gr and Lat, *P* narrates Andrew's return to Μυρμήκη to complete his mission there, just as the *Acts of Andrew and Matthias* promised he would. *P* also tells of Andrew's departure from the city with his disciples for Amasia, as in Gregory's epitome. *P* also knows that Andrew received by lot "the region of Pontus (or the Black Sea) and all of Achaea." The author may indeed have known the ancient *Acts of Andrew* directly, but seems rather to have known and conflated other Andrean literature and traditions with a version of the *Acts of Andrew and Matthias*. It is particularly disappointing that this manuscript so freely recasts its antecedents that it cannot be used with confidence in establishing the text.

The reconstruction of the *Acts of Andrew and Matthias* translated in this volume results from the application of the following criteria:

1. A reading is preferred when Gr and any representative of Lat agree.
2. When Gr and all representatives of Lat disagree, the most primitive readings of both text-types are recorded, either in the text or in the notes. Unless internal reasons dictate otherwise, the best reading of Gr is translated in the main text, the best reading of Lat in the note.
3. Readings from *P* are recorded only when they help adjudicate between *Gr* and *Lat*, or when the content of *P* is independently noteworthy.

The following sigla indicate the status of particular readings:

(. . .)	a lacuna (gap)
<xxx>	conjectural emendation
italics	a reading only in Lat

To avoid cluttering the translation with excessive bracketing, readings only in Gr are not specifically so identified.

Part II reproduces Gregory's Latin epitome along with parallels from several other sources. The *Epistle of Titus* (fifth century) alludes to the double wedding in GE 11 (see De Bruyne); the *Manichaean Psalm-Book* (fourth century?) alludes to the extinguished fire in GE 12 (see Allberry); and *P. Oxy.* 851 (fifth or sixth century), almost certainly a Greek fragment of the *Acts*, corresponds with a few lines in GE 18 (see Grenfell and Hunt). More instructive is a Sahidic Coptic excerpt calling itself ⲧⲡⲣⲁⲝⲓⲥ ⲛⲁⲛⲇⲣⲉⲁⲥ ("The Act of Andrew"—note the singular), conventionally known as *Papyrus Coptic Utrecht* 1. The first eight pages are lost, but the singular "Act" in the title suggests that this portion narrated only the content of the *Acts* parallel to the first few lines of GE 18. This missing fragment is therefore likely to have retained an episode that was suppressed by Gregory. Nevertheless, the manuscript as we have it has lacunae at several key places and the content of the rest is not easily harmonized with undisputed passages in the *Acts*.

The single most important parallel to Gregory for appreciating the general content of the *Acts* is a Βίος ("Life") written by a ninth-century monk, Epiphanius (PG 120.216–60). Among his sources he lists Clement of Rome (end of the first century), Evagrius of Sicily (ca. 536–600), and a catalogue of the apostles and of the seventy disciples falsely attributed to Epiphanius of Cyprus (see Flamion: 70–74). The reference to Clement presumably refers to the *Pseudo-Clementines* (Flamion: 74–75). Although this monk of Callistratus does not list the *Acts of Andrew* among his sources, he obviously knew a version of Andrew's passion and other sources whose content ultimately derived from the *Acts*.

 Determining how much of Epiphanius's material once appeared in the *Acts* is impeded by three major obstacles. First, Epiphanius gathered some of his information from local legends that may well have issued from the *Acts of Andrew* but whose origin can no longer be proved. Second, Epiphanius was not a historian but a panegyrist, and quite capable of fetching content from his private stock. Third, Albert Dressel based his 1845 edition on two manuscripts of questionable fidelity. Bonnet saw another manuscript differing considerably from Dressel's edition—one which still has not been edited or collated with others (see Flamion: 68–69). Nevertheless, one cannot afford to ignore Epiphanius's *Life* (= E) altogether.

Later in the ninth century, Nicetas the Paphlagonian memorialized Andrew in his own panegyric, conventionally referred to as *Laudatio* (= L), the bulk of which merely recasts Epiphanius's *Life* (Bonnet, 1895: 3–44; see Flamion: 57–62). Even so, readings from *Laudatio* are recorded insofar as they frequently preserve the text of Epiphanius more faithfully than the manuscripts of Epiphanius themselves.

Once Andrew arrives in Patras, Nicetas switches to a second source: a recension of the *Acts of Andrew* known also by the author of the *Martyrium prius* (= M, late eighth century; new text in Prieur: 675–703). This *Martyrium* alludes to the story of Matthew (as he is called) in "Myrmenis", and then states that the apostle traveled to Bithynia, Macedonia, and Achaea before arriving at Patras. It begins by narrating Andrew's ministry in detail, but only that portion after his arrival in Patras (see GE 22). In spite of its derivation from an intermediate recension, *Martyrium prius*—especially when compared with *Laudatio*—is now the most valuable witness to the episodes following Andrew's first arrival in Patras (Flamion: 62–69).

Narratio (= N, late eighth century) also parallels Gregory's epitome (Bonnet: 46–64). Its author knew some version of Andrew's passion as well as Andrean traditions from other sources, some of which may themselves have used the ancient *Acts*. The text of the passion is so close to that of Epiphanius as to suggest that the two authors both carefully recopied a common source or, more likely, that someone later touched up the passion in Epiphanius to make it conform with the *Narratio*.

Thus supplemented, Gregory's account sends Andrew from Myrmidonia to Amasia, where he heals a blind man (2), raises a dead boy (3), and vindicates a lad against his incestuous mother (4). In Sinope he heals a household (5), in Nicaea banishes roadside demons (6), and in Nicomedia brings another boy back to life (7), He then sails to Byzantium (8), disarms a gang of robbers in Thrace (9), and converts sailors on his way to Macedonia (10). In Philippi and Thessalonica he disrupts a double wedding (11), miraculously extinguishes a house fire (12), heals, revives, and exorcizes (13–17), convinces a soldier to bolt ranks (18), slays a monstrous serpent (19), and learns in a vision the circumstances of his martyrdom (20). From Macedonia Andrew goes to Patras, Achaea (21), where he converts Lesbius the proconsul (22), rescues a woman from a brothel (23), and raises up forty corpses from the sea (24). Andrew and Lesbius then travel through the Peloponnese while the apostle performs further healings and exorcisms (26–29). By the time he returns to Patras, the rogue Aegeates has become proconsul in Lesbius's place. Andrew heals the infirm, including Maximilla, wife of Aegeates (30–33).

Part III is an eclectic reconstruction of the Passion based on recensions in Greek, Latin, and Armenian. Before Prieur's and MacDonald's editions, all publications of the conclusion of the *Acts of Andrew* had relied on Flamion's reconstruction, pieced together from the *Narratio*; Epiphanius; *Martyrium prius*; the *Laudatio*; a Greek martyrdom from two divergent recensions conventionally known as the *Martyrium alterum* (= Ma); two mss, from the eleventh and fourteenth centuries, in Lipsius-Bonnet: 2/1. 58–64; an extensive Greek fragment, *Vaticanus graecus* 808 (= Vat., tenth or eleventh century) in Lipsius-Bonnet: 2/1. 38–45; and two Latin passions: *Passio* (= Ep) (Lipsius-Bonnet: 2/1. 1–37; on its likely composition in Latin, see Bonnet: 1894) and *Conversante et docente* (= Cd) (Bonnet, 1894). Flamion also drew on two notices from Evodius of Uzala that allude to content not expressed in the witnesses listed above.

New manuscript discoveries and renewed attention to the Armenian Passion (= Arm) render Flamion's reconstruction obsolete. The single most important witness to the Passion and our only witness to long sections of it is a Greek recension surviving in two manuscripts. This was discovered by Prieur and given preliminary publication by Theodore Detorakis (1981–82; = *HS*). An unpublished Greek manuscript (*Ann Arbor gr.* 36 = *AA*), though beginning only at chap. 51, shares many readings with *HS* and almost certainly is likewise derived from an early transmissional stratum. The Armenian Passion (translated by Thomas J. Samuelian) does not begin until chap. 47, but a comparison with *HS* and *AA* shows that it, too, was based on a reliable Greek version, perhaps on the *Acts* itself (see Chérubin Tchérakian: 1904; French translation in Leloir: 1. 228–57). At several points the Armenian alone appears to preserve original readings.

The Passion begins with Andrew healing the slave of Stratocles, Aegeates's brother (1–5); Stratocles converts (6–12). Maximilla, refusing to bed with Aegeates (13–16), bribes her shapely servant Euclia to sleep with him instead (17–22), but when Aegeates learns the truth he executes Euclia and entreats Maximilla to resume having sex with him (23–24). When she refuses, the proconsul imprisons the apostle, but the faithful find ways of sneaking into the prison to listen to him preach (25–50). Aegeates finally decides to crucify this destroyer of his home, and in order to prolong the torture he ties Andrew to the cross with ropes (51–54). The crowds successfully pressure Aegeates to release Andrew (59–60), but Andrew chooses rather to die (61–63). Maximilla and Stratocles bury him and devote themselves to holiness. Aegeates leaps to his death (64).

In addition to these three Parts of the *Acts of Andrew*, translations of other materials frequently associated with the *Acts* appear on pp 113–15: a quotation from Augustine; an expanded version of Andrew's address to his cross; and a further Coptic fragment.

THE ACTS OF ANDREW AND
CLASSICAL GREEK LITERATURE

Several aspects of the *Acts of Andrew* indicate that its author wanted to write a Christian *Odyssey*. The *Acts* begins with Andrew, the former fisherman, sailing with the aid of his god from Achaea to rescue Matthias from Myrmidons, Achilles's allies in Homer. Like Odysseus, the worst of the Myrmidons visit the netherworld and see the wicked punished. After raising the Myrmidons from the abyss, Andrew begins his journey back to Achaea, a journey replete with demons, storms, and a monstrous beast. Patras not only is near Ithaca, Odysseus's island home, it also allows for a play on the Homeric formula ἐς πατρίδα γαῖαν, "to the ancestral land." Andrew is tied to his cross like Odysseus to the mast, symbolizing the apostle's voyage to his true homeland. His soul "speeds toward things beyond time, beyond law, beyond speech, beyond body, beyond bitter pleasures full of wickedness and every pain." This use of the siren episode from the *Odyssey* correlates with contemporary allegories of Odysseus as a cipher for the soul seeking to return to its immaterial home beyond the imperiling sea of matter. (See, e.g., Numenius, *De antro nympharum* 34; Clement of Alexandria, *Prot.* 12; further, MacDonald, 1994).

Lesser characters in the *Acts of Andrew* also play roles mimetic of characters in the *Odyssey*. Aegeates, "the one from Aegae," is "like the raging sea" and functions as a counter-Poseidon, whose Homeric home is Aegae (*Iliad* 13.17–31; *Odyssey* 5.381). Maximilla, who prefers the attention of a rival to intimacy with her own husband, contrasts with Penelope. Whereas Penelope sequesters herself in her bedroom, keeping suitors in the hall, Maximilla welcomes "the brethren" into her bedroom to hear Andrew preach. Stratocles is a counter-Telemachus. At the beginning of the *Odyssey*, Telemachus ("Fighter-from-afar") is but a babe, but he matures thanks to instruction from the Achaean champions, and finally becomes a man when he joins his father in destroying the suitors. Conversely, Stratocles ("Famous at battle") appears in the *Acts of Andrew* first as a soldier on leave to study philosophy. By the end, he gives birth to his own inner fetus, takes on the demeanor of a slave, and forswears violence. The attentive reader may also find recastings of Achilles, Hector, Helen, Menelaus, Heracles, Zeus, Hera, Hephaestus, Ares, Dionysus, and several other gods and heroes. Not only is Andrew a Christianized Odysseus, he is also a Christianized Socrates, willingly going to his death while educating his comrades concerning his soul.

By means of this contrastive characterization, the *Acts of Andrew* replaces the ethically questionable traits of Homeric heroes with Christian virtues. Instead of Odysseus's wealth, sex, and violence, the heroes here represent poverty, chastity, and military disobedience. The author chose Andrew as the hero not because of a rich anterior tradition about the apostle, but because no apostle could better symbolize the new Odysseus than Peter's brother— Mr. Manliness (Ἀνδρέας / ἀνδρεία), the former fisherman who had brought Greeks to Jesus (John 12:22).

In addition to the *Odyssey* the author of the *Acts* imitated or alluded to several other works of Greek classical antiquity. The following list is not exhaustive, but it does include the most obvious echoes. Most entries contain references to particular works, though several connect Andrew's *Acts* with such mythological characters as Heracles, Achilles, Agamemnon, Iphigenia, and Orestes, who appeared in many ancient literary works but were not, like Achilles, blessed with a poet to enshrine their memories. The parallels between the Passion and Plato's Socratic dialogues are far more extensive than can be treated here (see MacDonald, *Christianizing Homer*, 218–73).

AAM 1–3. The Myrmidonian cannibals
    Circe the cannibal (*Odyssey* 10.206–43)
AAM 4–5. Jesus provides Andrew with a boat
    Athena provides Telemachus with a ship (*Odyssey* 2.292–419)

AAM 8. Andrew's "we-voyage"
  Odysseus's adventures at sea (*Odyssey* 5)
AAM 9. Captain Jesus
  Captain Odysseus (*Odyssey* 5.270–80)
AAM 16–18. Andrew awakes on the shores of Myrmidonia
  Odysseus awakes on the shores of Ithaca (*Odyssey* 13.116–313)
  Hermes meets Odysseus on his way to Circe (*Odyssey* 10.277–309)
AAM 19. Andrew's entry into the prison of the Myrmidons
  Priam's entry into the camp of Achilles (*Iliad* 24.440–79)
AAM 20–21. Andrew rescues Matthias and the other prisoners
  Odysseus rescues his crew (*Odyssey* 10.388–97)
AAM 22–23. The man who sacrificed his children
  Agamemnon, Iphigenia, and Orestes
AAM 25–26 and 28. The dragging of Andrew's body
  The dragging of Hector's body (*Iliad* 22)
AAM 27. The seal on Andrew's head
  The radiance of Achilles' head (*Iliad* 18–22)
AAM 29–31. Myrmidons drown in the flood
  Achilles' battle with the river (*Iliad* 21.211–382)
AAM 32–33. Andrew leaves Myrmidonia
  Priam leaves Troy (*Iliad* 24.161–364)
The Missing Tour of Hades
  Odysseus's Visit to the Netherworld (*Odyssey* 11)
GE 2. The blind seer of Amasia
  Tiresias, the blind seer (*Odyssey* 11.91–151)
GE 4. The youth accused of incest and punished as a parricide
  Oedipus's parricide and incest (Sophocles *Oedipus tyrannus*)
GE 5. Gratinus's son at a woman's bath
  Telemachus and Polycaste (*Odyssey* 3.401–79 and 15.195–214)
GE 6–7. Dog-demons and the slain youth
  Actaeon
GE 11. The double wedding at Philippi
  The double wedding at Sparta (*Odyssey* 4.1–67)
GE 12. Exochus
  Melampus (*Odyssey* 15.222–55)
GE 13. Carpianus and Adimantus
  Zeus and Sarpedon (*Iliad*)
GE 14. The raising of the strangled youth
  The rescue of Hector's corpse (*Iliad* 24)
GE 15. The cripple and his captives
  Hephaestus and his trap (*Odyssey* 8.266–366)
GE 16. Nicolaus's gift of horses and a carriage
  Menelaus's gift of horses and a chariot (*Odyssey* 4.589–619)

GE 18–19. Andrew's fights with wild animals
    The labors of Heracles
GE 20. John predicts Andrew's death
    Tiresias predicts Odysseus's death (*Odyssey* 11.119–37)
GE 21. Anthimus and the man who fell overboard
    Orpheus and Butes (Apollonius of Rhodes *Argonautica* 891–919)
GE 22. Mr. Goblet of Patras
    Dionysus of Thebes (Euripides *Bacchae*)
GE 23. Trophime and Callisto
    Atalanta and Aphrodite
GE 24 and 26. Philopater, Verus, Sostratus, and Leontius
    Orestes, Pylades, Agamemnon, and Achilles
GE 25. Calliope
    Circe (*Odyssey* 10.203–468)
GE 26. Sostratus and Leontius
    Agamemnon and Achilles
GE 27. Two men at a bath
    Heracles and Hylas (Apollonius of Rhodes *Argonautica* 1.1207–62)
GE 28. Nicolaus of Sparta
    Menelaus of Sparta (*Odyssey* 4)
GE 29. Antiphanes of Megara
    Heracles and Megara (Euripides *Heracles*)
GE 33. The leper at the harbor
    Philoctetes (Sophocles *Philoctetes*)
Pas 1. Aegeates, Maximilla, and Stratocles
    Odysseus, Penelope, and Telemachus (*Odyssey*)
Pas 2–5. The madness of Alcman
    The madness of Heracles (Euripides *Heracles*)
Pas 7–10 and 42–43. Andrew's midwifery
    Socrates' midwifery (Plato *Theaetetus* 149a–151b)
Pas 13–14. Aegeates' return to Patras
    Odysseus's return to Ithaca (*Odyssey* 22 and 23)
Pas 16–26. Maximilla rejects Aegeates' bed
    Penelope and Odysseus (*Odyssey* 22 and 23)
Pas 28–29. Andrew in prison
    Socrates in prison (Plato *Phaedo* 59d–60a)
Pas 29–34. Opened doors and veiled eyes
    Opened doors and sleeping guards (*Iliad* 24.440–79)
Pas 47–50. Andrew in prison
    Socrates in prison (Plato *Phaedo*)
Pas 51. The charges against Andrew
    The charges against Socrates (Plato *Apology* 24b and *Republic* 631e–
    632a)

Pas 54–55. Andrew's laughter on the cross
  Socrates' laughter before the hemlock (Plato *Phaedo*)
Pas 56–58. Andrew's cross beside the sea
  Odysseus's mast (*Odyssey* 12.153–200)
Pas 59. The outrage of the crowd
  The outrage of Socrates' friends (Plato *Phaedo* and Xenophon *Memorabilia* 1)
Pas 60–62. Andrew, tied to the cross, unties his soul from his body
  Socrates' eagerness to untie his soul from his body (Plato *Phaedo*)
Pas 63. Andrew's death
  Socrates' death (Plato *Phaedo* 117b–118a)

HOW TO USE THIS BOOK

warned: "If you deny the uniform of the king, they will punish you." Gregory's *Epitome* omits any trace of the demoniac's rejection of military service, but does state that the soldier was slain—not by Varianus but at the demon's departure. If one prefers the cause of death anticipated in the Coptic fragment, the story will have told of Varianus's arrival and the execution of the deserter. Andrew then raises him back to life, just as he does in the following chapter.

Editor's comments

18c Meanwhile, the proconsul arrived in a fit of rage, and even though he stood next to the holy apostle, he was unable to see him. ¹Andrew said, "I am the one you seek, proconsul."ⁿ

³Immediately his eyes were opened:ᵃ he saw him and said indignantly, "What is this insanity, such that you scorn our order and subject our subordinates to your authority? ⁴It is clear that you are a magician and a troublemaker. ⁵Now I will subject you to wild beasts for scorning us and our gods: you will see if the Crucified One you proclaim can rescue you."

⁶"Proconsul," said the blessed apostle, "you should believe in the true God,ᵃ and in his son Jesus Christ whom he sent, especially when you see one of your soldiers killed."

⁷The holy apostle prostrated himself for prayer, and after he had poured forth an extremely long prayer to the Lord, he touched the soldier and said, ⁸"Rise up! My God, Jesus Christ, whom I preach, awakens you." Immediately the soldier rose and stood up, whole.

⁹"Glory to our God!" shouted the people.

¹⁰"O people, don't believe," said the proconsul. "Don't believe the magician!"

¹¹"This is not magic," they cried, "but sound and true teaching!"

Acts of Andrew translation

18c:2 ⁿ → AAnMt 25:1
18c:3 ᵃCf. Mk 10:52; Mt 20:34; Lk 18:43

Cross references

18c:6 ᵃ → 12:6

18c:5 • *the Crucified One: crucifixus* here presumably translates Greek ὁ ἐσταυρωμένος, found as a christological title in, e.g., *Mart. Pol.* 17:2; Justin *Dial.* 137.1.
18c:6 • *the true God, and his son whom he sent: Deum verum et quem misit filium eius Iesum Christum,* apparently a recontextualization of John 17:3 Vg, which has *Deum verum, et quem misisti Iesum Christum.*
    especially . . . killed: Of course, if Varianus himself has killed the boy, this last clause would be Gregory's own formulation.

Notes on translation

18c:11 *P. Oxy. 851* (recto) ". . .] he said: 'Do as you wish.' The governor said to the chief-hunters, 'Bring me here'" (the final word is corrupt, but might have read "living" or "the stranger"); (verso) ". . .] 'Lord governor, this person is not a magician, but perhaps his God is great.'"

Notes on original language manuscripts

THE ACTS OF ANDREW AND MATTHIAS

1 At that time, all the apostles were gathered together in one place:ᵃ they divided the regions <of the world> among themselves by casting lots, so that each would leave for his allotted share. ²The lot fell to Matthiasᵃ to go to the city *called Myrmidonia.* ³The people of that city ate no bread and drank no water, but ate human flesh and drank human blood. ⁴They would seize all who came to their city, dig out their eyes, and make them drink a drug prepared by sorcery and magic. ⁵When forced by them to drink the drug, the victims' hearts became muddled and their minds deranged. ⁶*Now out of their minds and taken to prison, they would eat hay like cattle or sheep.*

2 So when Matthias entered the gate of the city <of> Myrmidonia, the people of that city seized him and gouged out his eyes. ²They made him drink the drug of their magical deceit, led him off to the prison, and gave him grass to eat.

³He ate nothing: his heart was not muddled and his mind was not deranged when he took their drug; but he prayed to God, crying: ⁴"Lord Jesus Christ, we have forsaken everything to follow you,ᵃ knowing that you help all who hope in you. Pay attention and see what they have done to your servant Matthias—they have nearly reduced me to the condition of beasts, as you fully know. ⁵So if you have determined that in my case the lawless people of this city shall devour me, I'll not try to escape this arrangement of yours.

1:1 ᵃCf. Ac 2:1

1:2 ᵃCf. Ac 1:23, 26

2:4 ᵃCf. Mk 10:28; Mt 19:27

2:5 • *arrangement:* οἰκονομία, often translated "dispensation" or "plan of salvation"; see also 17:3; 29:9; 30:6; AcAndPas 16:5.

1:1 *At that time:* GE "after the Lord's ascension"; M "after his ascension" (similarly O AS Syr Arm E L). *so that each . . .:* GE "the apostle Andrew was allotted to proclaim the Lord Jesus Christ in the province of Achaea"; cf. *Acts Phil.* 3 ("brother Andrew went to Achaea and all of Thrace") and M "by lot, Bithynia, Sparta, and Achaea went to Andrew." **1:2** *called Myrmidonia:* Gr "the region of the cannibals"; GE "the city of Myrmidonia"; M "the city of Myrmenis."

1:3 *water:* Grm "wine." *human blood:* C adds "In the middle of the city an earthen oven had been constructed, and, in addition, next to that oven was a trough. They used to slaughter people in the trough in order to collect the blood there. Next to that trough was another into which the blood that was sprinkled into the first trough [. . .] and flows as though it had been purified [. . .] for drinking."

2:7 ªCf. 30:4; Ps 37:21
ᵇCf. AJn 113

⁶But give me back, Lord, the light of my eyes, so that I can see what the lawless men of this city are undertaking against me. ⁷<Please> don't abandon me, my Lordª Jesus Christ, nor hand me over to this bitter death."

3:1 ªCf. AAnGE 28:15;
Rev 19:5
ᵇCf. Lk 18:42; Ac
22:13
ᶜCf. Mt 20:34; Lk
18:43
3:2 ªCf. 8:4; Gn 28:15
3:3 ªCf. Mt 28:20

3:4 ªCf. 19:9

3 As Matthias was saying this prayer, a light shone in the prison and a voice came out of the light, saying,ª "Beloved Matthias, receive your sight."ᵇ Immediately he got his sight back.ᶜ ²Again the voice came, saying, "Brace yourself, our Matthias, and do not be terrified, for I will never abandon you.ª ³I will rescue you from every danger—not only you but also all your brothers and sisters who are with you, for I am with you every hour and always.ª ⁴But remain here twenty-seven days for the benefit of many souls, and then I will send Andrew to you who will lead you out of this prison, not only you but also all who are with you."ª ⁵When the Savior had said these things, he again said to Matthias, "Peace be with you, our Matthias,"ª and he returned to heaven.

3:5 ªCf. 4:8; Jn 20:19,
21, 26

3:6 ªCf. 19:4; Ac 16:25

⁶Seeing this, Matthias said to the Lord, "May your grace stay with me, my Lord Jesus!" Then Matthias sat in the prison and sang.ª

⁷When the executioners came into the prison to carry the people away to eat, Matthias would shut his eyes so they would not notice that he could see. ⁸The executioners came to him, read the ticket on his hand, and said to each other, "In three days we will take this one too from the prison and slaughter him." (⁹They would indicate for everyone they caught the date of their capture, and they tied a ticket to their right hands so that they would know the completion of <their> thirty days.)

3:3 • *brothers and sisters* (ἀδελφούς): "brothers," but often used in an inclusive sense. The word is virtually a technical term for Christians, as already in the NT (e.g., Matt 18:15, 21; Rom 1:13; Jas 2:14–17), and in appropriate contexts is variously translated "brothers and sisters," "believers," and "fellow believers"; see AcAndGE 20:1, 3, 13; 24:26; 28:23; AcAndPas 5:5; 6:1; 9:1; 10:4; 15:4; 12:8; 13:1, 2, 8; 19:1, 2; 47:2; 50:9; 51:1; 53:17; 54:6; 55:1; 60:5; 64:3.

3:6 *and sang:* C adds "When the wicked and cruel executioners put them in prison they tied on each captive's hand a ticket, and on each ticket was written the number of the thirtieth day. Each day the executioners came to them in the prison and examined those written tickets. Whomever they discovered by means of this writing to have been shut up already for thirty days, like animals for fattening, they would at once remove those whose thirty days had ended, kill them, and prepare the flesh for their judges to eat and the blood as a beverage for drinking."

3:7 *he could see:* C adds "Indeed, when the ticket was taken from his hand, they could not detect that his eye(s) could see"; similarly B.

4 When twenty-seven days had elapsed since Matthias had been captured, the Lord Jesus appeared in *the city of Achaea* where Andrew was teaching, and said to him, ²"Get up and leave, go with your disciples *to the city called*ᵃ *Myrmidonia*, and bring Matthias out of that place, for in three days the citizenry will bring him out and slaughter him for their food."

³"My Lord," answered Andrew, "I cannot travel there before this three-day limit, so send your angel quickly to get him out of there. ⁴You know, don't you, Lord, that I too am fleshᵃ and cannot go there quickly. I don't even know the route there."ᵇ

⁵"Obey the one who made you," he told Andrew, "the one who could speak but a word and that city and all its inhabitants would be brought here. ⁶Yes, if I were to command the horns of the winds, they would drive it here. ⁷But you, get up early, go down to the sea with your disciples, and you will find a boat on the shore that you and your disciples should board.ᵃ ⁸Having said this, the Savior again said, "Peace to you, Andrew, and to those with you,"ᵃ and he went <back> into heaven.

5 Rising early in the morning, Andrew and his disciples went to the sea, and when he reached the shore he saw a small boat and, seated in the boat, three men. ²The Lord by his own power had prepared the boat. He himself was in the boat like a human captain, and he had brought on board two angels whom he had transformed to look like humans, and they were sitting in the boat with him.

³When Andrew saw the boat and the three men in it, he was exuberant. He went to them and said, "Brothers, where are you going with this little boat?"

⁴"We are going to the city *Myrmidonia*," answered the Lord.

⁵Andrew looked at Jesus but did not recognize him, because Jesus was hiding his divinityᵃ and appeared to Andrew as a human captain. ⁶"I too am going to the <city> of the <Myrmidons>, *Andrew answered, "so take us to this city, brothers."*

⁷"<Normally,> everyone wants to get away from that city," Jesus told him. "How is it you are going there?"

⁸"We have a small task to perform there, and we must finish it," Andrew answered. ⁹"So if you can, do us the favor of taking us to <the city Myrmidonia> where you too are now going."

4:2 ᵃCf. Jon 1:1 LXX

4:4 ᵃCf. ATh 1; APh 4
ᵇCf. Jn 14:5

4:7 ᵃCf. Jon 1:3 LXX; APe 3.5

4:8 ᵃCf. 3:5

5:5 ᵃ→ 10:2

4:2 *to the city called Myrmidonia*: Gr "to the region of the cannibals"; GE "Arise and go to the city Myrmidona."

5:4 *the city Myrmidonia*: Gr "the region of the cannibals"; so also in 5:6, 9.

¹⁰"*If it is so very necessary for you,*" Jesus answered, "board *this boat and travel with us.*"

6 "Young man," said Andrew, "I have to make something clear to you before we board your boat."

²"Say what you want," Jesus said.

³"Listen, brother: we have no fare to offer you,"ᵃ Andrew said, "and we have nothing to eat."

⁴"How then can you come on board, if you have no fare for us and nothing to eat?" Jesus asked.

⁵"Listen, brother," said Andrew to Jesus, "do not think that we'd withhold our fare from you as an act of arrogance. ⁶We are disciples of our Lord Jesus Christ, the good God. He chose us twelve and gave us this command: 'When you go to preach take on the road no money, no bread, no packsack, no sandals, no staff, and no change of tunic.'ᵃ ⁷So if you will do us the favor, brother, tell us right away. If not, let us know and we'll leave and find ourselves another boat."

⁸"If this is the command you have received, and if you are carrying it out," Jesus told Andrew, "board my boat joyfully. ⁹Actually, I would rather bring aboard my boat you disciples of the one called Jesus than those who offer me gold and silver—I like to think that I am fully worthy that the apostle of the Lord board my boat!"

¹⁰"Brother," responded Andrew, "allow me: May the Lord grant you glory and honor." Andrew and his disciples boarded the boat.

7 After boarding he sat down by *the sail of the boat,* and Jesus said to one of the angels, ²"Get up and go below to the hold of the boat: bring up three loaves, *and place them before all the brothers,* so that the men can eat in case they are hungry from having come to us after <so> long a trip." ³He got up, went below to the hold of the boat,ᵃ and brought up three loaves, just as the Lord had commanded him, and set out the bread for them.

⁴Then Jesus said to Andrew, "Brother, stand up with those in your party and take bread for nourishment to be strong enough to put up with the turbulence of the sea."

6:3 *nothing*: lit. "no bread"; so too in the next verse.
6:9 *I like to think that*: The phrase translates the simple explanatory particle γάρ; the hidden Jesus is of course secretly jesting.

6:10 *glory and honor: C* adds "and may he himself pilot you always, on the sea and everywhere."

7:1 *the sail of the boat: Lat* "the pilot"; *P* "opposite the pilot."

6:3 ᵃCf. Jon 1:3 LXX

6:6 ᵃCf. Mk 6:8–9; Mt 10:7–10; Lk 9:3; 10:4; APe 3.5

7:3 ᵃCf. Jon 1:5 LXX

[5]"My children,"[a] Andrew told his disciples, "we have experienced great generosity from this person, so stand up and take bread for nourishment, so that you can be strong enough to put up with the turbulence of the sea."

[6]His disciples could not respond to him with so much as a word; they were already seasick. [7]Then Jesus insisted that Andrew and his disciples take bread for nourishment.

[8]"Brother," said Andrew, <still> unaware that he was Jesus, "may the Lord grant you heavenly bread from his kingdom. [9]Just leave them alone, brother; you see that the servants are queasy from the sea."

[10]"Perhaps the brothers have no experience of the sea," Jesus told Andrew. "Ask them if they want to return to land and wait for you until you finish your task and return to them again."

[11]So Andrew asked his disciples, "My children, do you want to return to land and wait for me there until I finish the task I was sent to do?"

[12]"If we separate from you," they answered Andrew, "we may become strangers to the good things that you provided us. No, we shall be with you wherever you go."

8 Jesus said to Andrew, "If you are really a disciple of the one called Jesus, tell your disciples about the miracles your teacher did so that their souls may be joyful and they may forget the terror of the sea, because we're about to shove the boat off shore." [2]Jesus at once told one of the angels, "Cast off the boat," and he cast the boat off from land. [3]Jesus <then> went and sat at the rudder and piloted the craft.

[4]Andrew encouraged and strengthened his disciples, saying, "My children, you who have handed over your souls to the Lord, don't be afraid, for the Lord will never abandon us.[a] [5]At that time when we were with our Lord, we boarded the boat with him, and he lay silently on board in order to test us; he was not really sleeping. [6]A great wind arose, and the sea swelled such that the waves broke over the sail of the boat. [7]Because we were terrified, the Lord stood up and rebuked the winds, and calm returned to the sea.[a] [8]All things fear him, because they are his creations. [9]So now, my children, don't be afraid, for the Lord Jesus will never abandon us."

[10]As holy Andrew said this, he prayed in his heart that his disciples would be drawn off to sleep *and no longer be terrified by the tempest.* And as Andrew prayed, his disciples fell asleep.

7:5 [a]Cf. 27:3

8:4 [a] → 3:2

8:5–7 [a]Cf. Mk 4: 35–41; Mt 8:23–27; Lk 8:22–25

9:1 ªCf. Lk 7:40

9 Andrew turned to the Lord, still not knowing it was the Lord, and said to him, "*There is something I would like to say to you.*"ª

²"*Say what you wish,*" the Lord told him.

³"Sir, show me your sailing technique, *because from the moment I boarded until now I have constantly observed your piloting and I am astounded.* ⁴I have never seen anyone sail the sea as now I see you doing—I have sailed the seas sixteen times; this is my seventeenth, and I have never seen such skill. ⁵The ship actually responds as though it were on land. So, young man, show me your technique, for I eagerly desire to learn it."

⁶"We too have often sailed the sea and been in danger," Jesus told Andrew, "but because you are a disciple of the one called Jesus, the sea knew that you were righteous, and so it was still and did not lift its waves against the boat."

⁷Then Andrew cried out in a loud voice, "I bless you, my Lord Jesus Christ, that I have met a man who glorifies your name."

10:2 ªCf. 5:5; 12:4

10 "Tell me, disciple of the one called Jesus," Jesus asked Andrew, "why did the faithless Jews not believe in him and say that he was not God but a human? ²*How could a human do the miracles of God and his great wonders*? Make it clear to me, disciple of the one called Jesus, for we heard that he revealed his divinity to his disciples."ª

³"Brother," Andrew answered, "he did indeed reveal to us that he is God, so do not suppose he is a human, for he himself created human beings."

⁴"Why then did the Jews not believe?" Jesus asked. "Perhaps he performed no signs in front of them."

10:6 ªCf. Mt 11:5;
Lk 7:22
ᵇJn 2:1–1
10:7–8 ªCf. Mk
6:32–44; Mt 14:
13–21; Lk 9:10–17;
Jn 6:1–13

⁵"Haven't you heard about the miracles he performed before them?" answered Andrew. ⁶"He made the blind see, the lame walk, the deaf hear, he cleansed lepersª and changed water into wine.ᵇ ⁷He took five loaves and two fish, made a crowd recline on grass, and after blessing the food gave it to them to eat. ⁸Those who ate were five thousand men and they were filled. They took up their excess: twelve baskets of leftovers.ª ⁹And even after all these miracles they did not believe in him."

¹⁰"Perhaps he did these signs in front of the people but not before the high priests," Jesus told Andrew, "and for this reason they did not believe in him."

9:4 • *sixteen times* or "sixteen years" (ἑξκαιδέκατον).

10:3 *human beings:* Grm "the heaven and the earth and the sea and everything <in> them" (cf. Exod 20:11; Neh 9:6; Ps 146:6; Acts 4:24; 14:15; Rev 10: 6; 14:7).
10:10 *did not believe in him:* C "rose up against (B: did not accept) him."

11 "No, brother," answered Andrew, "he did them also before the high priests, not only publicly but also privately, and they didn't believe in him."

[2]"What kind of miracles did he do privately?" Jesus asked. "Tell me all about them."

[3]"You and your inquisitive spirit!" Andrew said. "Why are you testing me?"

[4]Jesus said, "By saying these things to you, disciple of the one called Jesus, I'm not testing you; quite the contrary: my soul's delighted, excited—not only mine, but every soul that hears about his wonders."

[5]"O child," Andrew said, "the Lord will completely fill your soul with joy and everything that's good, since you've asked me now to tell you the signs which our Lord did privately.

12 "When we twelve disciples went with our Lord into the temple of the gentiles, to have us recognize the devil's ignorance, when the high priests saw us following Jesus, they said to us, [2]'O you wretches, how can you walk with someone who says, "I am the son of God"? God doesn't have a son, does he? Who of you has ever seen God consorting with a woman? [3]Isn't this the son of Joseph the carpenter? Isn't his mother Mary, and his brothers James and Simon?'[a]

[4]"When we heard this, our hearts turned over. But Jesus, knowing that our hearts were giving way, took us to a desolate place, performed great signs before us, and demonstrated his divinity for all of us <to see>.[a] [5]So we said to the high priests, 'You come too, and see[a]—he's persuaded us!'

13 "And so it happened: the high priests went with us and went into the temple of the gentiles, and Jesus showed us the form of heaven, so that we should know *whether* it was real or not. [2]Thirty laypeople and four high priests went in there with us. [3]Looking to the right and left of the sanctuary, Jesus saw two sculpted *marble* sphinxes, *the very images of the cherubim, which the priests of the idols worship and adore*, one on the right and one on the left. [4]Jesus turned to us and said, 'Look! The replica of heaven, for these are similar to the cherubim and seraphim in heaven.' [5]Then Jesus looked at the sphinx on the right *side of the temple* and said to it, 'I tell you, model <of what> is in heaven, which the hands of artists sculpted, be

12:3 [a]Cf. Mk 6:3; Mt 13:55; Lk 4:20; Jn 6:42

12:4 [a] → 10:2

12:5 [a]Cf. Jn 1:39, 46

12:1 *our Lord . . . ignorance:* Lat "with him, where they made their idols public to us."

13:5 *come down:* Lat adds "for the Lord will give you a mouth to speak" (cf. Luke 21:15).

loosed from your place, come down: answer, and disgrace the high priests, and prove to them that I am God and not a human.'

14 "Right away, at that very moment, the sphinx leapt up *from its place*, acquired a human voice, and said, 'O those foolish sons of Israel, the blindness of their own hearts is not enough for them—they want to make others blind, just like themselves, by saying God is a human. [2]He it is who from the beginning formed humankind and gave his breath to everything, who moves everything immovable. [3]He it is who called Abraham, who loved his son Isaac, who returned his beloved Jacob to his land, *appeared to him in the desert, and made for him many good things*.[a] [4]He it is who led them out and gave them water from the gushing rock.[a] [5]He is the judge of the living and the dead.[a] [6]He it is who prepares marvelous things for those who obey him,[a] and prepares punishment for those who do not believe in him. [7]Don't suppose that I'm merely a marble idol: I tell you that the temples are more beautiful than your synagogue. [8]Stones we may be, but the priests gave us alone the name 'god,' and the very priests who conduct worship in the temple purify themselves for fear of the demons. [9]If they have sex with women, they purify themselves seven days, for fear they cannot enter into the temple because of us—and all because of the name they gave us: 'god.' [10]But when you fornicate, you take the law of God, go into God's synagogue, sit, read, and do not reverence the glorious words of God. [11]Therefore, I tell you that the temples will abolish your synagogues, so that they even become churches of the unique son of God.' Having said this, the sphinx was silent.

15 "'What the sphinx has said is true,' we told the high priests— 'even the stones tell you the truth and so put you to shame.'[a]

[2]"The high priests of the Jews answered, 'Look carefully and you'll see that this stone speaks by magic. You mustn't suppose that he's a god. [3]Had you tested what the sphinx said to you, you'd have known this, because you heard the stone claim that this is the one who spoke with Abraham. [4]Where did he find Abraham or see

14:3 [a]Cf. Gn 12:1–3; 22:2; 33:18; Exod 16

14:4 [a]Cf. Ex 17:1–7; Num 20:2–13
14:5 [a]Cf. Ac 10:42; 2 Tm 4:1; 1 Pt 4:5
14:6 [a]Cf. Mt 20:23; 25:34; 1 Cor 2:9

15:1 [a]Cf. Mt 3:9; Lk 3:8; 19:40

15:3–4 [a]Cf. Jn 8:56–58

15:4 • *a great many* translates the litotes "not a few" (οὐκ ὀλίγα).

14:1 *blind like themselves:* Lat "like us," i.e., like the blind idols (cf. Ps 115:5; 135:16; Wis 15:15).
14:2 *He it is . . . immovable:* Lat "For he is the God who made heaven and earth, the human in his image and likeness, and all the foundations of the earth." Cf. Gen 1:21–29; 2:7.

him? Since Abraham died a great many years <before> this person was born, how could he have known Abraham?"[a]

[5]"Once more Jesus turned to the sphinx and said to it, 'Why do these people not believe that I spoke with Abraham? [6]Go and enter the land of the Canaanites, go to the double cave in the field of Mambre where the body of Abraham lies[a] and outside the tomb call out: [7]"Abraham, Abraham, you whose body is in this cave, but whose soul is in paradise, thus says the one who molded humankind at the beginning, the one who made you his own friend:[a] [8]'Arise with your son Isaac and Jacob, and go into the temples of the Jebusites so that we can refute the high priests, and they may know that I knew you and you me.'"

[9]"Hearing this, at once the sphinx walked out before all of us, went into the land of the Canaanites, to the field of Mambre, and called out to the tomb, just as Jesus had commanded it. [10]Instantly the twelve patriarchs came out of the tomb alive, and said to it, 'To which of us were you sent?'

[11]"'I was sent to the three patriarchs for evidence,' the sphinx answered. 'But as for you, go and rest until the time of resurrection.'

[12]"Hearing this, they went into the tomb and slept.

[13]"But the three patriarchs went with the sphinx, came to Jesus, and refuted the high priests.

[14]"Then Jesus said to the patriarchs, 'Go to your places.' And they left at once. [15]Jesus turned to the sphinx and said, 'Go up to your place,' and immediately it arose and stood at its place.

[16]"Even though the high priests saw these things, they did not believe in him. [17]He showed us many other mysteries, which, should I narrate them to you, brother, you would hardly believe your ears."

[18]"I can take them," Jesus told him, "because when the prudent hear useful words, their hearts rejoice. [19]But when speaking with the perverted, you never persuade their souls—not until death."

16

When Jesus knew that the boat was nearing land, he laid his head[a] on one of his angels, was still, and stopped speaking with

15:6 [a]Cf. Gn 23:9, 17

15:7 [a]Cf. 2Chr 20:7; Is 41:8; Wis 7:27; Jas 2:23

16:1 [a]Cf. AAnPas 42:6; Mt 8:20; Lk 9:58

15:17 • *you would hardly . . . ears*: Literally, "you could not endure them."

15:19 *you never persuade their souls—not until death:* Lat "it is like someone who throws a pebble in a well."

16:1 *laid his head . . . Andrew:* Lat "positioned his head as though he were falling asleep."

Andrew. ²Seeing this, Andrew too laid his head on one of his disciples and fell asleep.

³Jesus knew that Andrew was asleep and said to his angels, "Spread out your hands, lift up Andrew and his disciples, leave, and place them outside the gate of the city *Myrmidonia*. ⁴Once you have set them on the ground, return to me."

⁵The angels did as Jesus commanded them: they lifted Andrew and his sleeping disciples, raised them up high, and brought them outside the gate of the city of the <Myrmidons>. ⁶After putting them down, the angels returned to Jesus, and then Jesus and his angels went back up into heaven.

17 Early in the morning Andrew woke, looked up, *and found himself* sitting on the ground. ²When he looked, he saw the gate of the city *Myrmidonia*. ³Looking around he saw his disciples sleeping on the ground, and he woke them up, saying, "Get up, my children, and know the great plan[a] that has been set before us. ⁴Learn that the Lord was with us in the boat and we did not know him, for he transformed himself into a captain in the boat. ⁵He humbled himself and appeared to us as a mortal in order to test us." ⁶When he had come to himself, Andrew had said, "Lord, I recognized your excellent speech, but I didn't recognize you because you didn't reveal yourself to me."

⁷"Father Andrew," his disciples said, "don't suppose that we were conscious when you spoke with him in the boat, for we were dragged off by a deep sleep. ⁸Eagles came down, carried away our souls, brought us to the heavenly paradise, and we saw great marvels. ⁹We saw our Lord Jesus sitting on a throne of glory and all the angels[a] surrounding him. ¹⁰We saw Abraham, Isaac, Jacob, all the saints, and David singing a psalm with his harp. ¹¹We saw you twelve apostles standing there before our Lord Jesus Christ, and outside twelve angels circling you. ¹²One angel stood behind each of you, and they were like you in appearance. ¹³We heard the Lord say to the angels, 'Listen to the apostles with regard to everything

17:3 a → 2:5

17:9 a Cf. Mt 19:28; 25:31

17:6 • *when he had come to himself* (ἐν ἑαυτῷ γενόμενος): The phrase is surely reminiscent of the so-called Prodigal Son's moment of conversion "when he came to himself" (Luke 15:17), though the Greek is very different (εἰς ἑαυτὸν δὲ ἐλθών).

16:3 *Myrmidonia:* Gr "of the cannibals."
16:5 *<Myrmidons>:* Gr "cannibals."
17:2 *city Myrmidonia:* Gr "that city."

17:8 *came down:* Grm add "from heaven."
17:9 *surrounding him:* C A Grp add "and singing hymns."

they ask of you.' [14]This is what we saw before you woke us, father Andrew, and they brought our souls back into our bodies."

18 When Andrew heard this he was exuberant that his disciples had been considered worthy[a] to see these marvels. [2]Andrew looked up into heaven and said, "Appear to me, Lord Jesus Christ, for I know you are not far from your servants. [3]Forgive me, for I saw you on the boat <only> as a human and spoke with you as with a human. Therefore, O Lord, reveal yourself now to me in this place."

[4]After Andrew had said these things, Jesus came to him appearing like a most beautiful small child and said, "Greetings, our Andrew."

[5]When Andrew saw him he fell to the earth, worshiped him, and said, "Forgive me, Lord Jesus Christ, for on the sea I saw you <only> as a human and spoke with you. [6]My Lord Jesus, what sin had I committed that caused you not to reveal yourself to me on the sea?"

[7]"You did not sin," Jesus said to Andrew. "I did these things to you because you said, 'I cannot travel to the city *Myrmidonia* in three days.' [8]I showed you that I can do anything and appear to each person in any form I wish. [9]Now stand up, go to Matthias in the city, and bring him and all those strangers who are with him out of the prison.[a] [10]And look, Andrew, before you enter their city I'm going to show you what you must suffer.[a] [11]They will shower you with many terrible insults, contrive tortures, scatter your flesh on the public avenues and streets of their city. [12]Your blood will flow on the ground like water. They will not be able to kill you, but they will devise many afflictions. [13]Stand firm, our Andrew, and do not respond in kind to their unbelief.[a] [14]Remember those many tortures my soul endured when they beat me, spat in my face,[a] and said, 'He casts out demons through Beelzebul.'[b] [15]Am I not able with the blink of my eyes to crush the heaven and the earth against those who sin against me? But I endured and forgave in order to provide a model also for <all of> you. [16]So now, our Andrew, if they inflict on you these insults and tortures, endure them, for there are those in this city who are about to believe." [17]After the Savior said these things, he went back into the heavens.

18:1 [a]Cf. Ac 5:41

18:9 [a]Cf. Jon 3:1–2 LXX

18:10 [a]Cf. Ac 9:16

18:13 [a]Cf. 26:3

18:14 [a]Cf. Mk 14:65; 15:19; Mt 26:67; 27:30; Lk 22:63; Jn 19:3
[b]Cf. Mk 3:22; Mt 9:34; 12:24, 27; Lk 11:15, 19

18:4 • *small child:* By contrast, the devil will appear as an old man (24:2).

18:5 *spoke with you:* Grp add "as with a human."
18:7 *Myrmidonia:* Gr "of the cannibals."
18:16 *there are those in this city who are about to be-* lieve: C "you will capture in your net many people of this city who will believe in me."

19:1 ªCf. Jon 3:3 LXX

19:3 ªCf. 29:5; AAnGE 9:2

19:4 ª → 3:6

19:5 ªCf. Rm 16:16; 1 Cor 16:20; 2 Cor 13:2; 1 Ths 5:26

19:8 ªCf. Mt 10:16; Lk 10:3

19:10 ªCf. 3:4

20:3 ªCf. AAnGE 18b:39

20:5 ªCf. Gen 3

20:7 ªCf. Gn 6:1–14

19 Andrew got up and went to the city with his disciples without anyone seeing him.ª ²They went to the prison, and Andrew saw seven guards standing at the door of the prison guarding it. He prayed silently, and the seven guards fell and died. ³When he came to the prison door, Andrew marked it with the sign of the crossª and it opened automatically. ⁴On entering the prison with his disciples, he saw Matthias sitting, singing by himself.ª

⁵When he saw Andrew, Matthias rose, and they greeted each other with a holy kiss.ª ⁶"O brother Matthias," Andrew said, "how is it that one finds you here? In three days they would have taken you out for slaughter, and you would have become food for the people of this city! ⁷But where are the great mysteries you were taught? Where are the marvels with which we were entrusted, any of which would shake heaven and earth if you were to narrate them?"

⁸"O brother Andrew," Matthias answered, "did you not hear the Lord say, 'Behold, I send you as sheep in the midst of wolves?'ª ⁹For as soon as they brought me into prison I prayed to the Lord, and he revealed himself to me, saying, 'Stand firm here for twenty-seven days, and then I will send you Andrew who will deliver you and everyone with you from the prison.' ¹⁰Now look, I see you just as the Lord said I would!ª So now, what should we do?"

20 Then Andrew looked into the middle of the prison and saw the prisoners naked and eating grass like dumb beasts. ²Andrew beat his breast and said to himself, "O Andrew, look and see what they have done to people like you, how they nearly reduced them to the state of irrational animals."

³Then Andrew began to rebuke Satan, saying to him, "Woe to you, Devil, enemy of God and his angels. These wretches and strangers did you no harm,ª so why have you brought this punishment on them? ⁴*O rogue*, how long will you make war with the human race? ⁵From the beginning you caused Adam to be expelled from paradise.ª ⁶God caused him to sow a diet of grain on the earth, but you turned his bread on the table into stones. ⁷Later, you

---

19:7 • *where are the great mysteries?* Andrew appears to berate Matthias for not using his spiritual powers to punish his captors and escape.

     shake heaven and earth: Here Andrew's counsel is *not* to invoke the power of God to "shake" the earth; later, in AcAndGE 4:15, Andrew's prayer appears to prompt an earthquake.

20:3 *Devil:* Lat adds "who waged such hostilities against the human race, cruel and perverse one." **20:5** *Adam:* Lat P and one other Gr ms add πρωτόπλαστον ("the first-formed"), used of Adam already in Wis 7:1; 10:1; likewise in early Christian writers, e.g., Irenaeus *Adv. haer.* 3.21.10 (*protoplastus*); Hippolytus *Comm. in Dan.* 4.11.5 (*PG* 11. 1829A); PsClemHom 18.13:6. **20:7** *the minds of the angels:* Lat "into the heart(s) of the sons of God."

sneaked into the minds of the angels, made them to be defiled with women, and made their unruly sons giants, so that they devoured the people of the earth, until the Lord raged against them and brought a flood on them in order to obliterate every structure the Lord had made on the earth. ⁸But he did not obliterate his righteous one,ᵃ Noah. ⁹Now you come to this city as well in order to make its residents eat humans *and to <drink> their blood* so that they too may end up accursed and destroyed. You are assuming that God will obliterate what he has molded. ¹⁰*Enemy!* Have you not heard that God said, 'I will never again bring a flood on the earth?'ᵃ If any punishment is prepared, it is for retaliation against you."

20:8 ᵃCf. AAnPas 51:6

20:10 ᵃCf. Gn 9:11

21 Andrew and Matthias then got up and prayed, and after the prayer Andrew put his hands on the faces of the blind men in the prison, and immediately they received their sight. ²He also put his hands on their hearts, and their minds regained human consciousness. ³Then Andrew said to them, "Stand up, go to the lower parts of the city, and you will find along the road a large fig tree. Sit under the fig tree and eat its fruit until I come to you. ⁴Should I delay coming there, you will find enough food for yourselves, for the fruit of the fig tree will not fail. ⁵No matter how much you eat, it will bear more fruit and feed you, just as the Lord commanded."

⁶"Come with us, our lord," the men said to Andrew, "so that the lawless men of this city won't see us again, lock us up, and inflict tortures on us more dreadful and numerous than what they have inflicted on us so far."

⁷"Go!" Andrew answered them. "For I tell you truly that as you go not even a dog will bark at you with his tongue."

⁸The men went off just as blessed Andrew had told them. The men whom Andrew released from prison numbered in all two hundred *forty-eight*, and the women forty-nine. ⁹He made Matthias go with his disciples out of the city toward the east. ¹⁰Andrew commanded a cloud, and the cloud lifted Matthias and Andrew's disciples and placed them on the mountain where Peter was teaching, and they stayed with him.

20:8 • *righteous* or "just one" (δίκαιος): The epithet is applied to Noah in Gen 6:9; Wis 10:4; Sir 44:17; and among early Christian writers by, e.g., Justin *Dial.* 138.1.

20:10 *If any punishment . . . you:* Lat "Whatever hostilities you now perform against the human race, similar torments are laid up against you for the day of judgment"; cf. Matt 25:41.
21:10 *disciples:* Eth names them "Rufus and Alexander"; cf. Mark 15:21; *Acts Pet. And.* 1.

22:1 ªCf. Jon 4:5 LXX

22 After Andrew left the prison, he walked about the city, and *by a certain street* he saw a pillar with a copper statue standing on it. He sat behind that pillar in order to see what would happen.ª ²When the executioners arrived at the prison to remove people for their food according to their daily custom, they found the doors of the prison opened and the *seven* guards lying dead on the ground. ³At once they went and told the rulers, "We found the prison opened, and when we went inside we found no one, except for the guards lying dead on the ground."

⁴When the rulers of the city heard these things, they said to each other, "What has happened? Have some people perhaps gone into the <city> prison, killed the guards, and released the prisoners?" ⁵So they commanded the executioners, "Go to the prison and bring those seven men so that we may eat them. ⁶Tomorrow, let's go and round up all the elderly of the city so that they can cast lots among themselves until the lots select seven. ⁷Let's slaughter seven each day, and they will be our food until we select some young men and appoint them to <our> boats as sailors. ⁸They can invade the neighboring territories and bring captives here for our food."

⁹The executioners went and brought out the seven dead men. ¹⁰Now an earthen oven had been erected in the middle of the city, and next to it lay a large trough where they used to put the people to death. ¹¹Their blood would flow into the trough, from which they would draw up the blood and drink it—so they brought the men and placed them in the trough. ¹²When the executioners lifted their hands over them, Andrew heard a voice saying, "Andrew, look at what is happening in this city."

¹³Andrew looked and prayed to the Lord, "My Lord Jesus Christ, <you who commanded> me to enter this city, <please> don't let the residents of the city do any harm, but let the swords fall from their lawless hands, *and may their hands be like stone.*" ¹⁴Immediately the swords fell from the executioners' hands, and their hands became stone.

¹⁵When the rulers saw what had happened, they cried, "Woe to us, for there are magicians here who even went into the prison and led the people out! Look—they have put these men too under

22:2 *daily:* καθημερινήν, in P and one other Greek ms (cf. 31:3); Grm "blessed" (μακαρίαν), perhaps indicating a cultic purpose.
22:6–8 C "Because that trough that preserves blood for us remains empty."
22:10 C places this description of the oven and trough at 1:3 (see note).

22:13 *Christ:* Lat adds "who created me in my mother's womb, who made me enter into the light, I implore you through your mercy."
22:15 *Look . . . magic spell:* Lat "And the guards are slain, and now they have petrified the hands of the executioners."

a magic spell. ¹⁶What should we do? Go now, and gather up the elderly of the city; we're hungry."

23 They went and rounded up *all the old people of the city*, and found two hundred seventeen. ²They brought them to the rulers, made them cast lots, and the lot fell on seven of the old people. ³One of those selected said to the attendants, "I beg you! I have a small son. Take him, slaughter him in my place, and let me go."

⁴The attendants answered him, "We cannot take your son unless we first discuss the matter with our superiors."

⁵The attendants went and informed the rulers, and the rulers answered the attendants: "If he gives you his son in his place, let him go."

⁶When the attendants came to the old man, they told him, and the old man said to them, "In addition to my son I also have a daughter. Take and slaughter them <both>, only let me go."ᵃ ⁷And so it was that he delivered up his children to the attendants for them to slaughter, *but they let him go unharmed.*

⁸As they went to the trough, the children wept together, and begged the attendants, "Please: don't kill us when we are so small, but let us reach full stature; then slaughter us." ⁹But the attendants did not listen to the children or have any mercy on them, but brought them crying and begging to the trough.

¹⁰As they brought them for slaughter, Andrew saw what was happening and cried. ¹¹He looked into heaven weeping and said, "Lord Jesus Christ, you listened to me in the case of the dead guards and did not let them be devoured. ¹²So now too, listen to me, so that the executioners may not bring death on these children: Loosen the swords from the hands of the executioners." ¹³Immediately the swords were loosened and fell from the hands of the executioners like wax in fire.

23:6 ᵃCf. 31:1

23:1 • *two hundred seventeen*, i.e., one month's supply: 7 x 31 = 217; Lat "207"; Syr "216."

22:16 *hungry:* Lat adds "because our food is gone."
23:2 *cast lots:* Lat adds "<to see> who would be their food and whose blood their drink."
23:5 C "Go and take his son and hang him on a scale. If he weighs more than the father, remove him and kill him for us. But if he weighs less, do not accept him. By doing this you will see if the younger weighs less."

23:8 *wept together:* Lat adds "threw themselves at the feet of the executioners."
Please: Lat P add "have mercy on our youth."
slaughter us: Grp (including P) add "It was customary in that city not to prepare the dead for burial, but to eat them" (similarly Syr and Eth).
23:13 *the executioners:* B "their swords melted and their hands withered."

[14]When the executioners saw what had happened, they were terrified. [15]But when Andrew saw, he gave glory to the Lord, because he had responded to him in every instance.

24 When the rulers saw all of this, they wept in great distress, saying, "Woe to us, for now we perish. What shall we do?"

24:2 [a]Cf. 18:4

[2]Then the devil came looking like an old man[a] and began to speak in the midst of them all: [2]"Woe to you, for now you are dying for lack of food. What good will sheep or cattle do you? They will never satisfy you. [3]*If you want my advice*, get up and search for a certain stranger here residing in the city named Andrew and kill him. [4]If you don't, he will not allow you to carry out this practice ever again, because it is he who released the people from prison. [5]Beware: the man is in this city, though you don't recognize him. So now, get up! Seek him out, so that at last you can gather your food."

[6]Andrew saw how the devil was speaking to the crowds, but the devil did not see blessed Andrew. [7]Then Andrew told the devil, "O most cruel Belial, opponent of every creature, my Lord Jesus Christ will lower you into the abyss."

[8]When the devil heard this he said, "I hear your voice, and I recognize it, but I don't know where you're standing."

[9]"Why were you nicknamed Amael?" Andrew asked the devil. "Was it not because you are blind, unable to see all the saints?"

[10]Hearing this, the devil said to the citizens, "Look around now for the one who is speaking with me, for he's the one!" [11]The citizens ran about, shut the city gates, and searched for the blessed one but did not see him.

[12]Then the Lord revealed himself to Andrew and said to him, "Andrew, arise and reveal yourself to them, so that they can learn the power of the devil who sways them."

25 So Andrew stood up in front of everyone and said, "Look, I am Andrew whom you seek."

24:1 • *What shall we do?* The rulers presumably fear revolt, since their means of feeding the population have been thwarted.

24:7 • *Belial* (ὦ Βελία): In the NT the title occurs only at 2 Cor 7:15 (Βελίαρ, v.l. Βελίαλ); it is of course frequent in the Qumran Dead Sea Scrolls.

25:1 • *Look, I am Andrew whom you seek:* ἰδοὺ ἐγώ εἰμι Ἀνδρέας ὃν ζητεῖτε, as in Acts 10:21 (Peter's speech to the messengers from Cornelius), except that in Acts the disciple is not named; see also John 18:4–7; AAnGE 18b:2.

24:2 *them all:* B "the elders of the city Marmedona."

24:9 *Amael:* Grp, perhaps rightly, "Samael," or "Satanael"; P "Satan."

²The crowds ran to him, grabbed him, and said, "What you have done to us we shall do to you." ³They debated among themselves, saying, "How shall we kill him?" They said to each other, "If we behead him, his death will not be agonizing for him." ⁴Still others said, "If we burn him with fire and give his body to feed our superiors, this death is not torturous <enough> for him."

⁵Then one of them, whom the devil had entered and taken possession of, said to the crowd, "As he has done to us, let us do to him. ⁶Let us invent the most heinous tortures for him. Let us go, tie a rope around his neck, and drag him through all the boulevards and streets of the city every day until he dies. ⁷When he is dead, <then> let's divide his body for all of the citizens and pass it out for their food."

⁸Hearing this, the crowds did as he had said to them. They tied a rope around his neck and dragged him through all the boulevards and streets of the city. ⁹As blessed Andrew was dragged, his flesh stuck to the ground, and his blood flowed on the ground like water. ¹⁰When evening came, they threw him into the prison and tied his hands behind him. He was utterly exhausted.

26 Early the next morning they brought him out again, tied a rope around his neck, and dragged him about. Again his flesh stuck to the ground and his blood flowed. ²Blessed Andrew wept and prayed, "My Lord Jesus Christ, come and see what they have done to *me* your servant. ³But I endure because of your command which you commanded me when you said, 'Do not respond in kind to their unbelief.' ⁴Now, Lord, observe how many tortures they bring upon me, for you, Lord, know human flesh. ⁵I know, Lord, that you are not far from your servants, and I do not dispute the command that you gave me; otherwise, I would have made them and their city plunge into the abyss. ⁶But I shall never forsake your command which you commanded me, even to the point of death, because you, Lord, are my help. Only don't let the enemy mock me."

⁷As blessed Andrew said these things, the devil was walking behind him saying to the crowds, "Slap his mouth to shut him up!"

⁸At nightfall they took Andrew, threw him again into the prison, tied his hands behind him, and left him again until the next day.

⁹Taking with him seven demons[a] whom blessed Andrew had cast out of the vicinity, the devil entered the prison, stood before

26:9 [a]Cf. AAnGE 6:1; Mt 12:45; Lk 8:2; 11:26

26:3 • *Do not respond in kind to their unbelief:* μὴ ποιήσῃς κατὰ τὴν ἀπιστίαν αὐτῶν; cf. 18:13; Acts Phil. 8; 15.25, 29, 31, 33, 34, 37.
26:4 • *for you, Lord, know human flesh:* Cf. John 2:24–25; Acts Phil. 4.
26:5 • Cf. Acts Phil. 15.26.

blessed Andrew, and jeered at him cruelly. [10]The seven demons and the devil taunted blessed Andrew: "Now you have fallen into our hands! [11]Where are your power, your awesomeness, your glory, and your grandeur, you who vaunt yourself up against us, dishonor us, tell our deeds to the people in every place and region—[12]you who make our temples deserted houses with the result that no sacrifices for our delight are offered up in them?[a] For this reason we will retaliate. [13]We will kill you just as Herod killed your teacher called Jesus."

27 The devil said to his seven wicked demons, "My children, kill him who dishonors us, so that at last all the regions will be ours." [2]Then the seven demons came and stood in front of Andrew, wanting to kill him. [3]But when they saw the seal on his forehead that the Lord had given him, they were afraid and were not able to approach him but fled. [4]The devil said to them, "My children, why do you flee from him and not kill him?"

[5]The demons answered the devil, "We cannot kill him, for we saw the seal on his forehead and were afraid of him, for we knew him before he came into this torment of his humiliation. [6]You go and kill him if you can; we can't obey you, lest God heal him and deliver us up to bitter tortures."

[7]"We cannot kill him," said one of the demons, "but come, let us mock him in this torment."

[8]The demons and the devil came to blessed Andrew, stood in front of him and mocked him, saying, "Look Andrew, you too have come to dishonorable shame and tortures. Who can rescue you?"

[9]After blessed Andrew heard these things he wept greatly, and a voice came to him, saying, "Andrew, why are you crying?" [10](The voice was the devil's—the devil had altered his voice.)

[11]"I cry," answered Andrew, "because my Lord commanded me, 'Be patient with them.' Had he not, I would have shown you <my power>."

[12]The devil answered Andrew, "If you have some such power, use it."[a]

[13]"Even if you kill me here," answered Andrew, "I will never do your will but the will of Jesus Christ who sent me.[a] [14]For this reason

26:12 [a]Cf. 1 Cor 10:20

27:12 [a]Cf. Mt 4:3, 6; Lk 4:3, 9

27:13 [a]Cf. Jn 4:34; 5:30

27:1 • *My children* (τεκνία μου): The devil relates to his demons in the same terms as Andrew and his disciples; see, e.g., 7:5, 11.

27:3 *seal:* Lat "sign of the cross" (similarly Eth); Lat again has "cross" for "seal" in 27:5.

then you do these things to me, so that I may neglect the command of my Lord; because if the Lord visits this city for my sake, then I will punish you as you deserve."

[15]When the seven demons heard these things, they ran off with the devil.

28 The next morning they again fetched Andrew, tied a rope around his neck, and dragged him. Again his flesh stuck to the earth, and his blood flowed on the ground like water. [2]As he was dragged, blessed Andrew <again> cried, saying, "Lord Jesus Christ, these tortures are enough; I am exhausted. Look at what the enemy and his demons have done to me. [3]Remember, O Lord, that you spent three hours on the cross and you weakened—you even said, 'My Father, why have you forsaken me?'[a] [4]Look, Lord, for three days I am dragged around in the boulevards and streets of this city. [5]Lord, especially because you know that human flesh is weak, command my spirit to leave me, my Lord, so that at last I may attain rest. [6]Lord, where are your words which you spoke to us to strengthen us, telling us, 'If you walk with me, you will not lose one hair from your head?'[a] [7]Therefore, Lord, look and see that my flesh and the hairs of my head stick to the ground, for I have been dragged around in heinous tortures for three days, and you, my Lord, have not revealed yourself to me to fortify my heart. I am utterly exhausted." [8]Blessed Andrew said these things as he was dragged about.

[9]Then a voice came to him in Hebrew, "Our Andrew, heaven and earth will pass away, but my words will never pass away.[a] [10]Therefore, look and see behind you what has happened to your fallen flesh and hair."

[11]Andrew turned and saw large fruit-bearing trees sprouting, and he responded, "I know, Lord, that you have not forsaken me."

[12]When evening came, they threw him into the prison. Already he was exceedingly weak. [13]The men of the city said to each other, "He will probably die during the night, for he is weak and his flesh spent."

29 The Lord appeared in the prison, and extending his hand he said to Andrew, "Give me your hand and stand up whole."

28:3 [a]Cf. Mk 15:34; Mt 27:46

28:6 [a]Cf. Lk 21:18; Ac 27:34

28:9 [a]Cf. Mk 13:21; Mt 24:35; Lk 21:33

28:10 • *look and see . . .:* Cf. *Acts Phil.* 15.37.
28:11 • *fruit-bearing trees . . .:* Cf. *Acts Phil.* 15.37, 42.

28:1 *dragged him:* C adds "through the streets and boulevards of the city."

28:12 *When evening came:* Grm add "they again lifted him up and . . ."

²When Andrew saw the Lord Jesus, he gave him his hand and stood up whole. ³He fell, worshiped him, and said, "I thank you, my Lord Jesus Christ."

29:5 ª → 19:3

⁴When Andrew looked into the middle of the prison, he saw a standing pillar and on the pillar rested an alabaster statue. ⁵He stretched out his hands and said to the pillar and the statue on it, "Fear the sign of the cross,ª at which heaven and earth tremble: ⁶let the statue sitting on the pillar spew from its mouth water as abundant as a flood, so that the residents of this city may be punished. ⁷Do not fear, O stone, or say, 'I am just a stone and unworthy to praise the Lord,' for in fact you too have been honored. ⁸The Lord molded us from the earth, but you are pure. Therefore, God gave to his people the tablets of the law made from you. ⁹He did not write

29:9 ª → 2:5

on gold or silver tablets but on tablets of stone. So now, O statue, carry out this plan."ª

¹⁰As soon as blessed Andrew had said these things, the stone statue spewed from its mouth a great quantity of water as if from a trench, and the water spilled up onto the ground. It was thoroughly brackish and consumed human flesh.

30
When morning came, the men of the city saw what had happened and began to run away, saying to themselves, "Woe to us, for now we die!" ²The water killed their cattle and their children, and they began to flee the city.

³Then Andrew said to the Lord, "Lord Jesus Christ, I already have

30:4 ªCf. 2:7

undertaken and performed this sign in this city. ⁴Don't abandon meª but send your archangel Michael in a fiery cloud and wall up this city, so that if any should want to get away they will not be able to pass through the fire."

⁵Immediately a cloud of fire came down and encircled the entire city like a wall. ⁶When Andrew learned that the planª had been

30:6 ª → 2:5

achieved, he blessed the Lord.

⁷The water rose to the necks of the men and was devouring them viciously. ⁸"Woe to us," they all cried and shouted, "because all these things have come upon us because of the stranger in pris-

---

30:4 • *in a fiery cloud* (ἐν νεφέλῃ πυρός): See also "a cloud of fire" (νεφέλη πυρός) in the next verse, and note on AcPaulThec 34:7. The incident perhaps recalls the disciples' suggestion in Luke 9:54 that Jesus "bid fire come down from heaven" on unbelieving Samaritans; cf. also Luke 12:49.

29:4 Grm add "Andrew scaled the statue."
29:10 *consumed human flesh:* C adds "most of the people and domestic animals"; B "from human to

cattle and every living creature"; AS "their children and their cattle" (similarly Syr).

on whom we handed over to tortures. ⁹What will we do? Let's go to the prison and free him, so that we don't die in this deluge of water. ¹⁰Let's all cry out, 'We believe in you, O God of this stranger! Take this water from us.'" ¹²So they all went out, crying in a loud voice, "O God of this stranger, remove this water from us."

¹²Andrew knew that their souls were submissive to him. Then blessed Andrew said to the alabaster statue, "Now at last stop spewing water from your mouth, for the time of rest has come. ¹³Look, I am leaving to preach the word of the Lord. I say to you, stone pillar, that if the inhabitants of this city believe, I will build a church and place you in it, because you did this service for me."

¹⁴The statue ceased flowing and no longer emitted water. Andrew left the prison, and the water ran from the feet of blessed Andrew. ¹⁵When the citizenry went to the doors of the prison, they cried out, "Have mercy on us, God of this stranger. Do not treat us as we treated this man."

31 The old man who had delivered up his children for slaughter in his place[a] came begging at the feet of blessed Andrew, "Have mercy on me."

²"I'm amazed," said holy Andrew to the old man, "that you can say, 'Have mercy on me,' when you had no mercy on your own children but handed them over in your place. ³Therefore I tell you, at that hour when the water recedes, you will go into the abyss—you and the fourteen executioners who killed people daily—and the lot of you will stay in Hades until I turn once again and raise you. ⁴So now, go into the abyss so that I may show these executioners the place of your murders and the place of peace, and to this old man the place of love and the surrender of his children. Now everyone follow me."

⁵As the men of the city followed him, the water divided before the feet of blessed Andrew until he came to the place of the trough where they used to put the people to death. ⁶Looking up to heaven,

31:1 [a]Cf. 23:6

31:3 • *daily* (καθ' ἑκάστην ἡμέραν): Cf. 22:2.
31:6 • *the earth opened . . . old man* (ἀνεῴχθη ἡ γῆ καὶ κατέπιε τὸ ὕδωρ σὺν τῷ γεραιῷ): This denouement recalls the providential frustration of the serpent/devil in Rev 12:16 (ἤνοιξεν ἡ γῆ τὸ στόμα αὐτῆς καὶ κατέπιεν τὸν ποταμὸν ὃν ἔβαλεν ὁ δράκων ἐκ τοῦ στόματος αὐτοῦ); see also AcAndGE 4:17.

30:15 *as we treated this man:* Grm "according to our unbelief" (cf. 26:3) and add "but remove this water from us."
31:2 *in your place:* Grm add "for slaughter."
31:5 *the water divided:* Lat adds "right and left"; cf.

Exod 14:21–29.
trough: Lat "mound."
31:6 *the old man:* Lat adds "who had betrayed his children."

blessed Andrew prayed in front of the entire crowd, and the earth opened and devoured the water along with the old man, and he and the executioners were carried down into the abyss.

⁷When the men saw what happened, they were terrified and began to say, "Woe to us, for this person is from God, and now he kills us for the torments which we inflicted on him. ⁸For look, what he said to the executioners and to the old man has happened to them. Now he will command the fire, and it will burn us."

⁹After hearing this, Andrew said to them, "My little children, do not be afraid; for I will not let even them stay in Hades. ¹⁰They went there so that you should believe in our Lord Jesus Christ."

32 Then blessed Andrew commanded all those who had died in the water to be brought to him, but they were unable to bring them because a great crowd of them had died—men, women, children, and animals. ²So Andrew prayed, and all revived.

³Later, he drew up plans for a church and had the church built on the <very> spot where the pillar in the prison had stood. ⁴After baptizing them, he handed on to them the commands of our Lord Jesus Christ, telling them, "Stand by these, so that you can know the mysteries of our Lord Jesus Christ, *for his power is great.* ⁵I will not hand them on to you now; instead, I am going to my disciples."

32:2 • *So:* τότε, usually translated "then"; but in the *Acts of Andrew*, as elsewhere (e.g., the Gospel of Matthew), it often functions as a simple connective or even causal conjunction.

32:2 • *prayed:* Neither Gr nor *A* provides content to this prayer, but from *C* AS one can reconstruct the following: "Lord Jesus Christ, send your Holy Spirit from heaven and raise up all the souls [*C*: who died] in this water, [*C*: from humans to sheep,] so that all may believe in your holy name."

and all revived: Photius reports that "he [Leucius] tells fabulous tales about irrational and childish resurrections from the dead of people and cattle and other domestic animals" (*Bibl.* cod. 114).

31:9 *for I will not let even them stay in Hades:* AS "for those who are now in this water will live again."
31:10 *Jesus Christ:* C adds "who has power in heaven, on earth, in the sea, and in the abyss."
32:3 *where the pillar in the prison had stood:* So P; B "in the place where the statue had been"; C "on that spot"; AS "on the spot where the column stood"; A "on the spot where those young men arose by baptism, even where the flood sprang forth." V says that the church was "in the middle of that city." No Greek, Latin, or Anglo-Saxon version says Andrew made good on his earlier promise to place the water-spewing statue in the church, but the Syriac does: "And they brought the pillar which had made the water flow and set it up in the church."
32:4 *Jesus Christ:* Lat adds "ordained one of their rulers as their bishop." V names the bishop Plato; A names him Platan. In P, this "Plato" plays an important role almost from the beginning of Andrew's ministry in Myrmidonia. See also the *Martyrdom of Matthew.*

[6]"We beg you," they all implored, "stay with us a few days, so that we may be sated from your fountain, because we are neophytes."

[7]Even though they begged him, he was not persuaded but said to them, "I will go first to my disciples." [8]And the children with the men followed behind crying and begging, and threw ashes on their heads.[a] [9]He was still not persuaded by them, but said, "I will go to my disciples, and later I will return to you"; and so he went on his way.

33 The Lord Jesus, having become like a beautiful small child,[a] came down and greeted Andrew, saying, "Andrew, why do you go away leaving them fruitless, and why do you have no compassion on the children following after you and on the men who implore, 'Stay with us a few days'? Their cry and weeping rose to heaven. [2]So now, turn back, go into the city, and stay there seven days until I strengthen their souls in the faith. [3]Then you may leave this city and you will go into the city of the barbarians, you and your disciples. [4]After you enter that city and preach my gospel there, you may leave them and again come into this city and bring up *all* the men in the abyss."

[5]So Andrew turned and <again> entered the city *Myrmidonia*, saying, "I bless you, my Lord Jesus Christ, who wants to save every soul, that you did not permit me to leave this city in my anger." [6]When he entered the city, they saw him and were jubilant.

[7]He spent seven days there teaching and confirming them in the Lord Jesus Christ. [8]At the completion of seven days, the time came for blessed Andrew to leave. [9]All *the people of Myrmidonia* were gathered to him, young and old, and sent him off, saying, "One is the God[a] of Andrew: the Lord Jesus Christ, to whom be glory and power forever. Amen."

32:8 [a]Cf. Jon 3:5 LXX

33:1 [a] → 18:4

33:9 [a]Cf. AAnGE 6:4; 18a:3; AAnPas 25:7; APaTh 9:2

The *Acts of Andrew and Matthias* stops here quite unexpectedly. Andrew was to have left the city to rejoin his disciples in the east (chapters 32 and 33, cf. 21), to have evangelized "the city of the

---

32:6 • *neophytes* (νεόφυτοι), a technical term for those newly converted; see also AcAndPas 12:8.

33:3 *into the city of the barbarians:* P "to the east, where your fellow apostle Matthew is."

33:9 *Amen.*: According to P, Bishop "Plato wrote everything from beginning to end."

barbarians," and to have returned to Myrmidonia to raise up the old man and the fourteen executioners who by then would have visited places of eternal bliss and torment (33). He does none of this in the best versions of the story now extant, but he presumably did in the original. One Greek recension (*Paris gr.* 1313) does indeed send Andrew back to raise the Myrmidons; but it is not certain that it retains the story from the ancient Acts. Again, according to the *Acts of Philip*, which is dependent on the *Acts of Andrew* for much of its narrative, Philip raises Snake-People (Ὀφιανοί) from an abyss where they had witnessed the eternal punishments of the wicked (*Acts Phil.* 15.32); likewise the *Acts of John Prochorus* 34–35 (Zahn), inspired by the *Acts of Andrew*, and AcThom 55–59.

Andrew's return may have been expunged because Manichaeans appealed to it to support their doctrine of reincarnation (Photius *Bibl.* cod. 179). In order to smooth over the difficulties created by Andrew's failure to return, later authors and copyists either omitted the promises or supplied the missing narrative, e.g., *Acts of Peter and Andrew* 1–3 and the Syriac and Ethiopic translations of the *Acts of Andrew and Matthias*. It is reasonable to assume that the original story continued as promised, with Andrew reconvening with his disciples and Matthias in the east, evangelizing in "the city of the barbarians," and returning to exhume the fifteen engulfed Myrmidons. From this point until the *Passion* the most reliable witness to the content of the Acts is the epitome by Gregory of Tours.

THE EPITOME BY GREGORY OF TOURS
and Related Materials

2 While he was walking with his disciples a blind man came up to him and said, "Andrew, apostle of Christ, I know that you are able to restore my sight, but that's not what I want to receive. [2]Rather, I ask that you order those with you to give me money for adequate clothing and food."

[3]Blessed Andrew said to him, "I know truly that this is not the voice of a human but of the devil, who doesn't want this man to regain his sight." [4]Turning around, Andrew touched his eyes, and immediately he received light and glorified God.

[5]Because the man's clothing was cheap and coarse, the apostle said, "Remove his filthy rags and give him new clothing." [6]<Soon> nearly all were stripping themselves, so the apostle said, "Let him have only the essentials." [7]So the man took the clothing, gave thanks, and returned to his home.

3 Demetrius, the leader of the community of Amasians, had an Egyptian boy whom he cherished with unparalleled love. [2]A fever overtook the boy, and he expired. [3]Later, when Demetrius heard of the signs the blessed apostle was performing, he came to him, fell at his feet[a] with tears, and said, "I am sure that nothing is <too> difficult for you, O servant of God. [4]Look, my boy, whom I love to an extraordinary degree, is dead. I ask that you come to my house and restore him to me."

[5]When the blessed apostle heard this, he was moved by his tears and went to the house where the boy lay. [6]After preaching at great length about what was needed for the salvation of the people, he turned to the coffin and said, "Lad, I tell you in the name of Jesus Christ, the Son of God, arise and stand up, healed."[a] [7]Immediately the Egyptian boy got up, and Andrew returned him to his master. [8]Then all the unbelievers believed in God and were baptized by the holy apostle.[a]

3:3 [a]Cf. 5:4; 11:7; 12:2; 15:8; 18a:6; 19:2, 14; 22:12; 24:11, 16; 27:2; 30:6

3:6 [a]Cf. 7:13

3:8 [a]Cf. Mt 8:1–13; Lk 7:1–10

2:1 • AcAndGE 1 tells the story of the Myrmidons, already reported in AcAndMat. In chap. 2 the setting, not mentioned until 3:1, is now Amasia. P reads: "When he reached Amasia, he kept silent."

3:1 *the community of Amasians:* P also sends Andrew off to Amasia after Myrmidonia.

4 A Christian youth named Sostratus came secretly to blessed Andrew and said, "My mother craved my beautiful looks and kept pestering me to sleep with her. ²Because I curse this unspeakable act, I ran away. But she, crazed with venom, went to the proconsul so as to put the blame on me for her own wrongdoing. ³I know that when accused I will make no defense, because I would rather relinquish my life than expose my mother's guilt. ⁴Now I admit this to you; perhaps you can agree to pray to the Lord for me, to prevent my being deprived of this present life even though I am innocent."

⁵While he was saying this, the proconsul's assistants came to arrest him. ⁶Then after making a speech, the blessed apostle got up and went with the lad.

⁷His mother strongly denounced him, saying, "Lord proconsul, I was barely able to escape being violated by this lad who disregarded the feelings of respect due to a mother and turned on me out of <his> debauchery."

⁸"Speak, boy, <and tell us> whether those things your mother has charged are true," the proconsul told him. He was silent. ⁹Again and again the proconsul interrogated him, but he gave no answer. ¹⁰Because he maintained his silence, the proconsul took counsel with his advisers about what to do.ᵃ Only now did the boy's mother begin to cry.

¹¹"Wretch!" the blessed apostle then addressed her. "You shed bitter tears for the disgrace you wished to inflict on your son, you whom desire so incited that in your blazing lust you didn't fear to lose your only son."

¹²When he had said this, the mother said, "Listen, proconsul. Ever since my son decided to commit this outrage, he has clung to this man and hasn't separated from him."

¹³Infuriated by these charges, the proconsul gave orders for the boy to be sewn into the leather bag for parricides and thrown in the river, and for Andrew to be incarcerated. ¹⁴Once the mode of his execution had been determined, the proconsul would destroy him as well.

¹⁵But as the blessed apostle prayed, there was a great earthquakeᵃ and frightful thunder. ¹⁶The proconsul fell from his seat, and everyone else was sprawled on the ground. Lightning struck the boy's mother; she withered up and died. ¹⁷Then the proconsul fell at the feetᵃ of the holy apostle and said, "O servant of God, have

4:10 ᵃCf. Ac 24:25; APaTh 17:5; ATh 141:8

4:15 ᵃCf. AAnMt 19:7

4:17 ᵃ → 3:3
ᵇ → AAnMt 31:6

4:1–19 • Presumably these events, too, take place in Amasia.

mercy on those who are perishing; otherwise the earth will swallow us up."[b]

[18]When the blessed apostle prayed, the earthquake stopped;[a] the lightning and the thunder were quiet. [19]Then he went around to those lying about terrified and raised them all up healthy. [20]The proconsul received the word of God,[a] believed in the Lord with his whole house, and they were baptized[b] by the apostle of God.

5 While being washed in a women's bath, the son of Gratinus of Sinope was tortured senseless by a demon. [2]Gratinus sent a letter to the proconsul asking that he prevail on Andrew to come to him, because he was gravely ill with a fever, and his wife was swollen with dropsy. [3]At the proconsul's request, Andrew got into a carriage and went to the city.

[4]When he arrived at the home of Gratinus, the evil spirit threw the boy into convulsions, and the boy fell at the apostle's feet.[a] [5]Andrew rebuked him: "Depart from God's servant, O enemy of the human race!"[a] Immediately he cried aloud and came out of him.[b]

[6]Andrew went to Gratinus's bed and said, "Your grave illness is quite appropriate: you left your own marriage bed and slept with a prostitute. [7]Get up in the name of the Lord Jesus Christ, stand up whole, and sin no more, lest you incur a worse ailment."[a] He was healed.

[8]To the woman he said, "O woman, the lust of the eyes has deceived you, so that you too leave your husband and sleep with others." [9]And he said, "Lord Jesus Christ, I entreat your kind mercy that you may listen to your servant and be ready, so that if this woman returns to the lewd filth which she formerly practiced, she will never be healed. [10]O Lord, by whose power future events are known, if you know that she is able to abstain from this disgrace, let her be healed at your command." [11]When he had said this, she passed liquids and was healed, along with her husband.

[12]Then the blessed apostle broke bread and gave it to her. When she had given thanks, she took it and believed in the Lord with her whole house.[a] [13]Thereafter neither she nor her husband perpetrated the abominations they had committed before.

[14]Later, Gratinus sent lavish gifts to the holy apostle at the hands of his servants. Afterwards he followed along with his wife; they fell

4:18 [a]Cf. Ps 106:30

4:20 [a]Cf. 10:3; 12:7; 13:3; 15:16; 18c:13; 19:2; 20:11; 21:2, 5; 22:20; 24:1, 13; 27:10; 29:16; 30:5, 15; → APaTh 5:1
[b]Cf. 5:12; 22:19; Ac 18:8

5:4 [a] → 3:3

5:5 [a]Cf. 7:8; 27:7; 29:19
[b]Cf. Mk 1:23–26; 9:20–27; Lk 9:38–42

5:7 [a]Cf. Jn 5:14

5:12 [a] → 4:20

5:1 • *Gratinus*, or possibly "Cratinus."
5:8 • *lust of the eyes:* Lat. *concupiscentia oculorum*, as in 1 John 2:16 Vg for ἡ ἐπιθυμία τῶν ὀφθαλμῶν.

before him and asked him to receive their gifts. [15]"My dear friends," he told them, "I can't accept these things; rather, they are yours to expend for the poor." He accepted nothing they offered.

6 After this,[a] he left for Nicea, where there were seven demons[b] lingering among the roadside tombs, who stoned passers-by in broad daylight and had already killed many <of them>. [2]As the blessed apostle approached, all the residents came to meet him on the way carrying olive branches, and they praised him: "Our salvation is in your hands, O man of God." [3]They described the entire situation.

[4]The blessed apostle said, "If you believe in the Lord Jesus Christ, the Son of God Almighty, with the Holy Spirit—one God[a]—you will be freed by his help from this demonic infestation."

[5]"We do believe in the one you have preached," they cried, "and we will obey your command, providing we are freed of this scourge."

[6]He thanked God for their faith and ordered the demons to present themselves before all the people; they came out in the form of dogs.[a] [7]The blessed apostle turned to the people and said, "Here they are—the demons who afflicted you. [8]If you believe that in the name of Jesus Christ I can command them to leave you, declare it here, in front of me."

[9]"We believe that Jesus Christ whom you preach is the Son of God," they cried.

[10]Then blessed Andrew commanded the demons: "Go to arid and barren places,[a] harm absolutely no one, and enter no place where the name of the Lord is invoked until you receive your due punishment of eternal fire."

[11]When he said these things, the demons growled and vanished from the eyes of those present: the population was freed. [12]The blessed apostle baptized them and installed Callistus as their bishop, a wise man who guarded blamelessly[a] what he had received from the teacher.

7 Later, when he approached the gate of Nicomedia, a dead man was being carried out of the city on a bier.[a] [2]His elderly father, sup-

6:1–11 [a]Cf. Mk 5:1–20; Mt 8:28–34; Lk 8:26–39
6:1 [b] → AAnMt 26:9

6:4 [a] → AAnMt 33:9

6:6 [a]Cf. 7:6

6:10 [a]Cf. Mt 12:43–45

6:12 [a]→ AAnPas 12:1

7:1 [a]Cf. Lk 7:11–17

6:12 • *bishop* (*episcopus*): This is the only place in GE or in undisputed sections of the *Acts of Andrew* where the apostle installs a bishop.

6:1–12 This story also appears in N 4.

ported by the hands of slaves, was scarcely able to pay for the funeral. ³His mother, bent over with age, her hair unkempt, followed the corpse wailing: "Woe is me, for I have lived so long that I am spending for my son's funeral what I had saved for my own."

⁴As they followed the corpse, screaming and mourning these and related misfortunes, the apostle of God arrived and, moved by their tears he said, ⁵"Please tell me what happened to this boy for him to have departed from this light."

⁶They were afraid to answer, but from the servants the apostle heard this: "When this youth was alone in his bedroom, all of a sudden seven dogs[a] rushed in and attacked him. He was savagely mangled by them, fell, and died."

7:6 [a]Cf. 6:6

⁷Then the blessed apostle sighed, raised his eyes toward heaven, and spoke through his tears: "Lord, I know that the attack was the work of the demons that I expelled from Nicea. ⁸I now ask you, O gracious Jesus, to revive him, so that the enemy of humankind[a] may not rejoice at his destruction."

7:8 [a] → 5:5

⁹When he had said this, he asked the boy's father, "What will you give me if I restore your son to you healthy?"

¹⁰"I have nothing more valuable than he. If he revives at your command, I will give him to you."

¹¹Again the blessed apostle raised his hands to heaven and prayed, "O Lord, I ask that the lad's breath return, so that by his resuscitation all may turn to you from forsaken idols. ¹²May his revival cause the salvation of all the lost, so that they may no longer be subject to death but win eternal life by having been made yours." The faithful responded, "Amen."

¹³Turning to the coffin he said, "In the name of Jesus Christ, get up and stand on your feet."[a]

7:13 [a]Cf. 3:6

¹⁴To the astonishment of the people he got up at once, and all present shouted with a loud voice, "Great is the God Christ, whom his servant Andrew preaches."

¹⁵The boy's parents gave their son many gifts which he offered to the blessed apostle, but Andrew accepted none of them.[a] ¹⁶He did take the boy to travel with him all the way to Macedonia, and taught him with saving words.

7:15 [a]Cf. 15:17

8 Leaving there, the Lord's apostle boarded a ship and sailed the Hellespont to get to Byzantium. ²A storm arose on the sea, a strong wind pressed down on them, and the ship foundered. ³At last, just when everyone was expecting to perish, blessed Andrew prayed to

8:4 ªCf. Mt 8:23–27;
Lk 8:22–25

the Lord, commanded the wind, and it was silent: the raging waves of the sea became placid, and there was calm. ⁴Having been saved from the immediate crisis,ª they reached Byzantium.

9 Proceeding from there so as to go to Thrace, they came upon a crowd of men a long way off with swords drawn, and brandishing spears as if they intended to attack. ²When the apostle Andrew saw them, he made the sign of the crossª against them and said, "I pray, O Lord, that their father who incited them to do this may fall. ³May they be thrown into disorder by divine power, so that they cannot harm those who hope in you."

9:2 ª → AAnMt 19:3

⁴As he said this, an angel of the Lord passed by with great splendor, touched their swords, and they fell sprawling on the ground. ⁵The blessed apostle passed by with his entourage unscathed, for the entire throng threw away their swords and adored him. ⁶Then the angel of the Lord departed from them in a great bright light.

10 The holy apostle arrived at Perinthus, a Thracian coastal city, and there found a boat about to leave for Macedonia. ²Again an angel of the Lord appeared to him and commanded him to board the boat. ³As he preached the word of Godª on board, a sailor and all who were with him believed in the Lord Jesus Christ, and the holy apostle glorified God that even on the sea there was someone to hear his preaching and to believe in the Son of God Almighty.

10:3 ªCf. 4:20; →
APaTh 5:1

11 There were two brothers at Philippi, one of whom had two sons, the other two daughters; both were rich, for they were of the highest nobility. ²One said to the other, "Look, we both have vast wealth, and there is no one in the city worthy of breeding with our clan. ³Come, let's merge our families into one: let my sons marry your daughters, so that we can more easily consolidate our wealth." ⁴The speech pleased his brother, and once the pact was made they secured the deal with an earnest sent by the boys' father.

⁵When the date for the wedding had been set, the word of the Lord came to them, saying, "Do not marry your children until my servant Andrew comes, for he will show you what you should do." ⁶<But> the nuptial chamber had already been prepared, the guests called, and all the wedding provisions were at the ready.

8:4 • *they reached Byzantium:* GE says nothing about Andrew's mission in Byzantium, but later tradition claims that when he arrived "he built a church there and ordained Stachys, one of the seventy disciples" (*N* 8). This tradition lies behind the Byzantine claim that Andrew had established its apostolic pedigree.

⁷Three days later, the apostle arrived. When they saw him they were jubilant, ran to him with wreaths, fell at his feet,ᵃ and said, ⁸"O servant of God, having been warned about you, we have been waiting for you to come and tell us what we should do. ⁹We got word to stall for you, and were told that our children should not be married before you arrived."

11:7 ª → 3:3

¹⁰Then the face of the blessed apostle shone like the sunᵃ to such a degree that all were amazed and honored him. ¹¹The apostle told them, "No, my little ones! Don't be led astray! Don't deceive these young people in whom the fruit of justice might appear! ¹²Rather, repent, for you have sinned against the Lord by wanting to unite blood relatives in marriage. ¹³It is not that we forbid or shun weddings—from the beginning God commanded the male and the female to be joined togetherᵃ—but we do condemn incest."

11:10 ªCf. Mt 17:2; Rev 1:16; 10:1

11:13 ªCf. Gn 2:24

¹⁴When he said this, their parents were disturbed and said, "Sir, we beg you to entreat your God for us, for we did this crime unwittingly."

¹⁵When the young people saw that the face of the apostle shone like the face of an angel of God,ᵃ they said, "Your teaching is great and untainted, blessed man, but we didn't know it. ¹⁶Truly, we now recognize that God speaks through you."

11:15 ªCf. 18a:6; 26:7; Ac 6:15; APaTh 3

¹⁷The holy apostle said to them, "Keep uncontaminated what you hear, so that God may be with you, and so that you may receive interest from your wealth—that is, everlasting life which never ends."

¹⁸When the apostle had said this and blessed them, he was silent.

12 At Thessalonica there was a young man, exceedingly noble and rich, named Exochus. ²Without his parents' knowledge he came to the apostle, fell at his feet,ᵃ and asked, "O servant of God, please show me the way of truth, because I recognize that you are a true servant of him who sent you."

12:2 ª → 3:3

11:11 • *fruit of justice* or "fruit of righteousness"; the Latin *fructum iustitiae* translates καρπὸς δικαιοσύνης, as in the Vg of Phil 1:11; Jas 3:18; cf. Heb 12:11. The phrase, which occurs in the LXX (see Prov 3:9; 1:10; 13:2; Amos 6:2; Hos 10:12), appears in AcPaulThec 4:4.
11:1–18 • The *Epistle of Titus* also refers to this story: "At last, when Andrew arrived at a wedding, he, too, to demonstrate God's glory, disjoined men and women whose marriages had been arranged and taught them to continue being holy as singles." The foiled wedding in AcThom 4–16, which may have been inspired by this story in the *Acts of Andrew*, likewise opposes marriage absolutely. It would therefore appear that the story in the ancient *Acts of Andrew* prohibited marriage itself, not merely incest.

12:6 ªCf. 12:18; 14:4
ᵇCf. 16:8; 1Ths 1:9–10

³So the holy apostle preached to him the Lord Jesus Christ. ⁴The youth believed and attached himself to the holy apostle, forgetting about his parents and altogether disregarding his financial affairs.

⁵When his parents inquired about him, they learned that he was staying with the apostle in Philippi. ⁶They brought gifts with them and begged the lad to abandon him, but he refused, saying, "If only you did not own these riches, so that by knowing the creator of the world, the true God,ª you might rescue your souls from the wrath to come!"ᵇ

12:7 ª → 4:20

⁷The holy apostle came down from the third story and preached the word of Godª to them. ⁸When they would not listen, he went back to the boy and shut the doors of the house. ⁹They got together an armed band and came to set fire to the house where the youth was, saying, "Let the lad perish who forsook his parents and his native land." ¹⁰They brought out bundles of stakes, reeds, and torches and began to ignite the house.

¹¹As the fire grew, the youth grabbed a small flask of water and said, "Lord Jesus Christ, by whose hand the nature of all the elements holds together, who moistens the parched and parches the moist, who cools what burns and ignites what has been snuffed

12:12 ªCf. Rv 3:15–16

out: ¹²Extinguish these flames, so that these people may not be lukewarm toward youª but may be set on fire for the faith." ¹³When he had said this, he sprinkled the water from the small flask, and immediately the entire fire was controlled so that it was as if it had never burned.

¹⁴When the boy's parents saw this, they said, "Look, our son already has been turned into a sorcerer." ¹⁵They brought out a ladder and intended to scale up to the third story to slay them by sword, but the Lord blinded them so they could not see the ladder's ascent.

¹⁶Because they persisted in this perversity, a citizen named Lysimachus said, "Men, why do you give yourselves to this futile task? Don't you recognize that God fights for these men? ¹⁷Stop this foolishness; otherwise the wrath of heaven will consume you."

12:18 ªCf. Ac 7:54
ᵇ → 12:6

¹⁸At these words, everyone was cut to the heartª and said, "The god those men worship and whom we tried to oppose is the true God."ᵇ

¹⁹By the time they had said this, nightfall had come. Suddenly a light shone, so that everyone could see. ²⁰They went up to the

---

12:10 • *to ignite the house*: The *Manichaean Psalm-Book* refers to this story. In a list of apostolic sufferings it is stated of Andrew that "they set fire to the house beneath him" (142.20).

place where the apostle of Christ was and found him praying. [21]Prostrate on the floor they cried out, "We ask you, sir, to pray for your servants who have been deceived by error." [22]Everyone was so repentant that Lysimachus said, "Truly Christ, whom his servant Andrew preaches, is the Son of God."[a] [23]Then the apostle raised them up and strengthened them in the faith; only the lad's parents did not believe.[a]

[24]They returned to their homeland cursing the youth and handed over all their belongings to the public authorities. Fifty days later, in the space of an hour, they both died. [25]Then, because all the men of the city loved this youth for his goodness and gentleness, they turned over to him from the public treasury his entire patrimony. (He possessed all that his parents had owned.) [26]Not even then did he separate from the apostle, but spent the income from the estate on the needs of the poor and the care of the indigent.

13 The youth asked the blessed apostle to set out with him for Thessalonica. [2]When they arrived there everyone swarmed to him, for they were glad to see the boy. [3]Then, when everyone was gathered at the theater, the boy preached to them the word of God,[a] so that the apostle did not need to speak. [4]The crowd was amazed at the boy's insight and cried out: "Save the son of Carpianus, our fellow citizen, for he is gravely ill; then we will believe in the Jesus you preach."

[5]The blessed apostle said to them, "Nothing is impossible for God.[a] [6]Bring him here to us, and the Lord Jesus Christ will heal him so that you may believe."

[6]His father then went to his house and said to the boy, "Today you will be healed, my beloved Adimantus"—that was the boy's name.[a]

[7]"My dream has indeed come true," he told his father, "because in a vision I saw this man restoring me to health."

[8]When he had said this, he put his clothes on, got up from his cot, and proceeded to the theater so quickly that his parents could not follow. [9]Falling at the blessed apostle's feet, he gave thanks for his restored health. [10]The crowd was stupefied at seeing him walk after twenty-three years,[a] and they glorified God, saying, "No one equals Andrew's God!"

14 One of the citizens, whose son had an impure spirit, asked the blessed apostle: "Please heal my son, man of God, for he is deep-

12:22 [a]Cf. Mk 15:39; Mt 27:54

12:23 [a]Cf. Jn 9:18–23

13:3 [a] → 4:20

13:5 [a]Cf. Lk 1:37

13:6 [a]Cf. 15:12; 24:17; AAnPas 4:4

13:10 [a]Cf. 15:12

ly troubled by a demon." [2]Foreseeing his impending expulsion, the demon led the boy to a secluded room and strangled him, wringing out his life with a noose.

[3]When the boy's father found him dead he cried—there was no stopping him—and he said to his friends, [4]"Take the carcass to the theater: I am sure that the stranger who proclaims the true God[a] can revive him."

14:4 [a] → 12:6

[5]When the lad had been carried out and placed in front of the apostle, the father related <to him> how the boy had been killed by the demon, and said, [6]"Man of God, I believe that through you he can arise even from death."

[7]The apostle turned to the crowd and said, "How will it benefit you, men of Thessalonica, if you see this done but still don't believe?"

[8]"Man of God," they said, "be assured that if he is raised we will all believe."

[9]When they had said this the apostle said, "Lad, in the name of Jesus Christ get up!" He got up at once.

[10]The entire crowd was amazed and cried out: "Servant of God, that's enough! All of us now believe in the God you preach." [11]They led him out to the house with torches and lamps (it was already past nightfall) and brought him inside his house, where for three days Andrew taught them the essential things about God.

15 A man from Philippi named Medias, whose son was seriously crippled, came to the apostle and said, [2]"I beg you, man of God, restore my son to me, for his body is crippled." He wept profusely as he spoke.

15:3 [a]Cf. Mk 5:36; Lk 8:50; ATh 21:6

[3]The blessed apostle wiped his cheeks, stroked his head, and said, "Be comforted, son. Only believe and your desires will come to pass."[a] [4]Then, seizing his hand, he went to Philippi.

[5]When he entered the city gate, an old man ran to him pleading for his children; Medias had forced them into confinement for unspeakable immorality, and they were indeed festering with sores.

[6]The holy apostle turned to Medias and said, "Listen, mister, you beg for your son to be healed, yet at your own home you hold in shackles people with rotting flesh. [7]If you want your prayers to come before God, first release the chains of those who suffer, so that your son too may be freed of his disability. I see that your cruelty impedes my prayers."

15:8 [a] → 3:3

[8]Medias then fell at his feet,[a] kissed him, and said, "I will free these two, and seven others unknown to you, so that my son may

be healed." [9]He ordered them arrayed before the blessed apostle, who laid hands on them, washed their wounds for three days, restored their health, and gave them <their> freedom.

[10]The next day Andrew said to the boy, "Get up in the name of the Lord Jesus Christ, who sent me to cure your infirmity." [11]He took his hand, lifted him up, and immediately the lad straightened up and walked, magnifying God. [12](The name of the lad who had been crippled for twenty-two years[a] was Philomedes.)[b]

[13]"Andrew, servant of God," shouted the crowd, "heal our sick!"

[14]The apostle told the lad, "Go to the houses of the sick and command them to rise up in the name of Jesus Christ who healed you."

[15]To the crowd's astonishment, he went off to the houses of the sick and restored them to health by invoking the name of Christ. [16]Then all the people believed, offered him gifts, and asked to hear the word of God.[a] [17]The blessed apostle preached the true God[a] but accepted no gifts.[b]

16 Later, a citizen named Nicolaus displayed a gilded carriage with four white mules and four white horses and offered them to the blessed apostle, saying, [2]"Take these, servant of God, for I found none of my possessions dearer than these; only let my daughter, plagued by a most terrible disease, be healed."

[3]The blessed apostle smiled and said to him, "Yes, I can receive your gifts, Nicolaus, but not these visible ones. [4]For if you offer the most precious things in your home for your daughter, how much more would you owe for your soul?[a] [5]Here is what I long to receive from you: that your inner self recognize the true God,[a] its maker and the creator of all; that it reject the earthly and crave the eternal; [6]that it neglect the fleeting and love the everlasting; that it deny what is seen and, by contemplation, cast spiritual glances at what is not seen. [7]When you have become alert to these things by means of trained perception, you will merit the attainment of eternal life and your daughter's restored health, and still more that you may enjoy in her the delights of eternity."

[8]By saying this he persuaded everyone to forsake idols and to believe in the true God.[a] [9]He healed Nicolaus's daughter from her illness, and all praised him, while reports of his miracles on behalf of the sick spread throughout Macedonia.

15:12 [a]Cf. 13:10
[b] → 13:6

15:16 [a] → 4:20
15:17 [a] → 12:6
[b]Cf. 7:15

16:4 [a]Cf. Mk 8:37; Mt 16:26

16:5 [a] → 15:7

16:8 [a]Cf. 12:6; 1Ths 1:9–10

16:3 • *smiled* (*subridens*): Smiling often indicates special knowledge or foresight; see also AcAndPas 3:4; 55(5):2; and further refs. at AcPaulThec 4:1.

17:1 ᵃCf. 27:2; Mt 8:29; Mk 1:24; Lk 4:34

17 On the following day, while Andrew was teaching, a young man cried out with a loud voice: "What do you have to do with us, Andrew, God's servant? Have you come here to chase us from our haunts?"ᵃ

²The blessed apostle called the youth to himself and said, "Tell me, contriver of crime, what is your work?"

³"I have inhabited this boy from his youth," he said, "and thought I'd never leave him. ⁴But three days ago I heard his father telling a friend, 'I will go to Andrew, God's servant, and he will heal my son.' ⁵Now I have come so as to desert him in your presence, because I fear the tortures you inflict on us." ⁶Having said this, he lay on the ground at the apostle's feet and left the boy, who was healed, got up, and gave glory to God.

17:7 ᵃCf. Ac 13:26; →
AAnPas 44:4
ᵇ → 12:6

17:8 ᵃCf. Mk 12:34;
Mt 22:46; Lk 20:40

⁷God displayed his grace through the holy apostle such that everyone voluntarily came to hear the word of salvationᵃ and said, "Tell us, man of God, who is the true Godᵇ in whose name you cure our sick?" ⁸Even philosophers would come and debate with him: no one could oppose his teaching.ᵃ

18a When these things had been done, an opponent of apostolic preaching arose and went to the proconsul Varianus, saying, ²"A troublemaker has arisen in Thessalonica, preaching that the temples of the gods must be destroyed, the rites rejected, and all decrees of ancient law struck down. ³He also preaches that only

18a:3 ᵃ → AAnMt
33:9

one Godᵃ should be worshiped, whose servant he declares himself to be."

⁴When the proconsul heard this, he sent infantry and cavalry to make Andrew appear before him. ⁵When they came to the gate, they determined in which house the apostle was staying. ⁶But on

18a:6 ᵃ → 11:15
ᵇ → 3:3

18a:1 • *When these things had been done:* What Gregory briefly narrates here probably occupied eight pages at the beginning of *Papyrus Coptic Utrecht* 1 (*PCU*). The singular "act" in the title of the document, the *Act of Andrew* (ⲧⲉⲡⲣⲁϫⲓⲥ ⲛ̄ⲁⲛⲇⲣⲉⲁⲥ), suggests that it told but one story: Andrew's confrontation with Varianus and the demoniac (cf. the Coptic *Act of Peter* [BG 8502.4], which likewise contains only one episode).

apostolic preaching: dictatio apostolica, presumably for τὸ ἀποστολικὸν κήρυγμα. By the late second century this was probably a technical term for primitive Christian teaching. It appears in the title of Irenaeus's treatise *The Demonstration of the Apostolic Preaching*; though this work survives only in an Armenian translation, its Greek title is given in Eusebius *Hist. eccl.* 5.26.

18a:4 • *before him:* Originally, Varianus may have directed his venom at Andrew not for berating or otherwise condemning pagan religion, as Gregory says, but for converting the proconsul's wife and repelling her from his bed. Later, almost in passing (see 19:12–13), Gregory discloses that Varianus's wife traveled with Andrew and even raised a dead man to life.

entering and seeing his face shining brilliantly,[a] they fell at his feet terrified.[b] [7]Then the blessed apostle told his audience what had been told the proconsul concerning him. [8]The crowd came with swords and clubs[a] wanting to kill the soldiers, but the holy apostle restrained them. [9]When the proconsul came and did not find the apostle in the city where he had expected to find him, he roared like a lion and sent twenty additional soldiers.

18a:8 [a]Cf. Mk 14:43;
Mt 26:47

The next episode is best represented by *Papyrus Coptic Utrecht* 1. This ms, comprised of fragments of a Coptic translation from Greek, and entitled "The Act of Andrew," provides a fuller treatment of this narrative at this point than Gregory of Tours. The first eight pages of the papyrus no longer exist, but the singular "Act" in the title indicates that it told one story only, apparently the conversion of Varianus's wife (see 19:1–2) and the proconsul's violent response. The context immediately preceding page 9 evidently told of four soldiers from Varianus arresting some of Andrew's followers.

18b . . .] the apostle. When Andrew, the apostle of Christ, heard that they had arrested those who were in the city because of him, he got up, went out into the middle of the street, and told the believers that there was no reason to conceal who they were.

[2]While the apostle spoke these words, there was a young man among the four soldiers in whose body a demon was hidden. [3]When that young man came before the apostle Andrew he cried out, "Varianus, what have I done to you that you should send me against this religious man?" [4]When the youth had said this, the demon threw him down[a] and caused him to froth at the mouth. [5]His fellow soldiers seized him and continued to [. . .] him.

18b:4 [a]Cf. Mk 1:26;
Lk 4:35

[6]But Andrew took pity on the youth and said to his fellow soldiers, "Are you not ashamed in my presence at seeing your nature rebuke you? [7]Why do you remove the prize-money, so that he cannot appeal to his king in order to receive help for finding the strength to fight against the demon hidden in his limbs? [8]Not only is he making an appeal for this, but he is speaking the language of

18a:9 • *twenty*: PCU speaks of only four soldiers; see 18b:2.
18b:1 • *the believers* (ΝΕϹΝΗΥ): "brothers," doubtless for ἀδελφοί; see note on AcAndMt 3:3.

the palace, so that his king may hear him at once. [9]For I hear him saying, 'Varianus, what have I done that you would send me out against this religious man?'" The apostle Andrew [. . .

In the missing six to eight lines Andrew apparently turns to the demoniac and addresses the demon. The demon seems to have begged Andrew to do nothing rash.

[10]" . . .] against me, for this act I have committed I did not commit on my own, but I was forced to do it. I will tell you the whole cause of the situation: [11]This young man whose body is convulsed has a virgin sister who is a great devotee of asceticism. [12]I tell you, honestly, that she is near to God because of her purity, her prayers, and her love. [13]Now, to tell it without elaboration, there was someone living next door to her house who was a great magician. It happened like this: [14]One evening, the virgin went up on her roof to pray;[a] the young magician saw her at prayer, and Semmath entered into him to fight with this great ascetic. [15]The young magician said to himself, 'Even though I have spent twenty years under my teacher before acquiring this ability, this now is the beginning of my career. [16]If I don't overpower this virgin, I will not be able to do anything.' [17]So the young magician conjured up some great supernatural forces against the virgin and sent them after her. [18]When the demons left to tempt her or to win her over, they pretended to be her brother and knocked at the door. [19]She got up and went downstairs to open up, supposing that it was her brother. [20]But first she prayed fervently, with the result that the demons became [. . .] <they> fell down and flew away [. . .] <the young> man [. . .]"

Two pages are missing, but it would appear that the magician, frustrated by his inability to overpower the virgin, uses his powers against the soldier, this time with success. On learning of her

18b:14 [a]Cf. Ac 10:9

18b:11 • *devotee of asceticism* (ⲁⲑⲗⲉⲧⲉⲥ = ἀθλήτης): Literally, "athlete"; so also in 18b:14 Cf. AcThom 39; 50; 85.

brother's condition, the virgin goes to her friend Eirusia for solace and guidance. The demon continues his story.

"...] [21]The virgin wept before Eirusia, but Eirusia said to the virgin, 'Why are you crying? Don't you know that those who come to this place cannot cry? [22]For this is the place [...] now these powers [...] come after you.' [23]Eirusia told her, 'Why are you crying, while the grief [...]. [24]Now then, if you're crying because of your brother, because a god [...] with him, tomorrow I will send him to the apostle Andrew so that he may heal him— [25]not only so that I'll bring him back to his senses, but so that I'll have him arm himself for the palace.'"

[26]When the demon had finished saying these things, the apostle said to him, "How did you learn about the hidden mysteries of the height? [27]Once they throw a soldier out of the palace, it is forbidden him to know the palatial mysteries; so how would he know the hidden mysteries of the height?"

[28]The demon told him, "I came down into this night, into this young man, while a power of the height entered into [...] friend [fem.] of the virgin going from him in [...] while she moves from [...] there. [29]The friend <of the virgin> said to her, '<Grief> touches me so that [...]. Tonight <the great> power from the height came down; it did [...] which I said [...] but when [...] know these, [....

In the missing lines, the demon presumably continues to explain how he learned about "the mystery of the height." It would appear that the legitimate heavenly power that had "entered" into Eirusia revealed these heavenly mysteries to the virgin, but the demon overheard them.

[30]<Andrew said,> "Why, then, do you not tremble when you speak of the mysteries of the height? [31]I tremble completely in all my limbs and I glorify the Receiver,[a] who comes after the souls of the

18b:31 [a]Cf. Jn 14:3

18b:31 • *the Receiver:* The Greek word παραλήμπτηρ is retained in the Coptic. This is not a standard early title for Christ; its meaning ranges from "reprehender" to "inheritor."

18b:36 ᵃCf. Mt 25:6

saints. ³²Athletes of virtue, you have not competed in vain. ³³Look: the Judge prepares the imperishable crown for you. ³⁴Warriors, you have not acquired weapons and shields or endured warfare in vain. ³⁵The King has prepared the palace for you. ³⁶Virgins, you have not guarded purity and endured in prayers in vain, your lamps glowing at midnight until this voice comes to you: 'Arise, go out to meet the bridegroom!'"ᵃ

³⁷When the apostle had said these things, he turned to the demon and said to him, ³⁸"It is now time for you to come out of this young man, so that he may arm himself for the heavenly palace."

18b:39 ᵃCf. AAnMt 20:3

³⁹"Truly, man of God," said the demon to the apostle, "I never harmed any of his limbsᵃ because of the holy hands of his sister, so now I will leave this young man to whose limbs I have done no violence whatsoever." ⁴⁰After he had said these things, the demon <left the young man>.

⁴¹When he had [. . .] the young man [. . .] of the military and <threw it> in front of the apostle, saying, ⁴²"Man of God, I spent twenty coins to obtain these items of this temporary uniform, but now I want to give all that I own to obtain these items of the uniform of your God."

⁴³"You unfortunate child!" his fellow soldiers told him. "If you deny the uniform of the king, they will punish you."

18b:45 ᵃCf. 1 Tim 1:17; APa 11.2:7

⁴⁴The young man said to them, "I am indeed unfortunate because of my previous sins. ⁴⁵Would that my punishment were only for denying the uniform of this king and not for despising the uniform of the King of the ages!ᵃ ⁴⁶You fools! Don't you see what sort of man this is? There is no sword in his hand nor any instrument of war, and yet these great acts of power issue from his hand."

The Act of Andrew

This abrupt ending leaves the reader to assume that Varianus would punish the soldier for desertion, just as the soldiers had

---

18b:33 • *the imperishable* (or "unfading") *crown:* Coptic ⲡⲉⲕⲗⲟⲙ ⲛ̄ⲁⲙⲁⲣⲁⲛ-ⲧⲓⲛⲟⲛ, reflecting τὸν ἀμαράντινον στέφανον (see 1 Pet 5:4). The phrase is often connected with martyrdom, and recurs, e.g., in AcThom 158:8 (also as a variant in 142:4); *Acts Eupl.* 2, where Euplus receives "*the unfading crown from Christ our God*"; *Acts Matt.* 24, where Matthew is greeted in heaven by "twelve men . . . with *golden and never-fading crowns* (ἀμαραντίνους καὶ χρυσοὺς στεφάνους) on their heads" (cf. Rev 9:7).

18b:41 • *the young man [. . . :* The lost line or lines probably narrated the young soldier's stripping off his uniform.

18b:45 • *King of the ages:* This title appears in Tob 13:6, 10; *1 Enoch* 9.4 (Greek Syncellus fragment); in early Christian writings, e.g., 1 Tim 1:17; Rev 15:3 (v.l.); *1 Clem.* 61.2.

warned: "If you deny the uniform of the king, they will punish you." Gregory's *Epitome* omits any trace of the demoniac's rejection of military service, but does state that the soldier was slain—not by Varianus but at the demon's departure. If one prefers the cause of death anticipated in the Coptic fragment, the story will have told of Varianus's arrival and the execution of the deserter. Andrew then raises him back to life, just as he does in the following chapter.

18c Meanwhile, the proconsul arrived in a fit of rage, and even though he stood next to the holy apostle, he was unable to see him. ²Andrew said, "I am the one you seek, proconsul."ᵃ

³Immediately his eyes were opened:ᵃ he saw him and said indignantly, "What is this insanity, such that you scorn our order and subject our subordinates to your authority? ⁴It is clear that you are a magician and a troublemaker. ⁵Now I will subject you to wild beasts for scorning us and our gods: you will see if the Crucified One you proclaim can rescue you."

⁶"Proconsul," said the blessed apostle, "you should believe in the true God,ᵃ and in his son Jesus Christ whom he sent, especially when you see one of your soldiers killed."

⁷The holy apostle prostrated himself for prayer, and after he had poured forth an extremely long prayer to the Lord, he touched the soldier and said, ⁸"Rise up! My God, Jesus Christ, whom I preach, awakens you." Immediately the soldier rose and stood up, whole.

⁹"Glory to our God!" shouted the people.

¹⁰"O people, don't believe," said the proconsul. "Don't believe the magician!"

¹¹"This is not magic," they cried, "but sound and true teaching!"

18c:2 ᵃ → AAnMt 25:1
18c:3 ᵃCf. Mk 10:52; Mt 20:34; Lk 18:43

18c:6 ᵃ → 12:6

18c:5 • *the Crucified One: crucifixus* here presumably translates Greek ὁ ἐσταυρωμένος, found as a christological title in, e.g., *Mart. Pol.* 17:2; Justin *Dial.* 137.1.

18c:6 • *the true God, and his son whom he sent: Deum verum et quem misit filium eius Iesum Christum,* apparently a recontextualization of John 17:3 Vg, which has *Deum verum, et quem misisti Iesum Christum.*

especially . . . killed: Of course, if Varianus himself has killed the boy, this last clause would be Gregory's own formulation.

18c:11 *P. Oxy. 851* (recto) ". . .] he said: 'Do as you wish.' The governor said to the chief-hunters, 'Bring me here'" (the final word is corrupt, but might have read "living" or "the stranger"); (verso) ". . .] 'Lord governor, this person is not a magician, but perhaps his God is great.'"

18c:13 ᵃ → 4:20

¹²"I will hand this man over to the beasts and will write Caesar about you, so that you may die shortly for despising his laws," said the proconsul.

¹³But they, so eager to stone him, said, "<Go ahead:> Write Caesar that the Macedonians received the word of God, detest idols, and worship the true God!"ᵃ At which the enraged proconsul returned to the praetorium.

¹⁴The next morning he sent wild animals into the stadium and ordered the blessed apostle dragged and flung into it. ¹⁵They seized him, dragged him by the hair, beat him with clubs, threw him into the arena, and dispatched a ferocious, horrible boar. ¹⁶The boar circled God's saint three times—yet did him no harm. ¹⁷When the crowd saw this, they gave glory to God.

¹⁸The proconsul again gave orders, this time that a bull be released, led in by thirty soldiers and provoked by two beast-fighting gladiators. ¹⁹It did not touch Andrew, but ripped the gladiators into pieces, gave a roar, and fell dead. ²⁰Immediately the people shouted: "Christ is the true God!" ²¹When this happened, an angel of the Lord was seen descending from heaven who comforted the holy apostle in the stadium.

²²Seething with rage, the proconsul at last ordered a fierce leopard sent in. ²³When dispatched, the leopard ignored the people, leapt onto the proconsul's throne, seized his son, and strangled him. ²⁴The proconsul was so overtaken by insanity that he felt no pain and said nothing whatever about these events.

²⁵The blessed apostle then turned to the people and said, "Realize now that you worship the true God, whose power has overwhelmed the beasts and about whom the proconsul Varianus still knows nothing. I will revive his son in the name of Christ whom I preach, so that you can more easily believe, and so that his thickheaded father may be embarrassed."

²⁷For a long time he prayed, stretched out on the ground; and then, taking the corpse's hand, he awakened him. ²⁸When the people saw this, they magnified God and would have killed Varianus, but the apostle would not allow it. ²⁹Varianus left for his praetorium, befuddled.

19 After this, a young man who already had been with the apostle told his mother what had happened, and summoned her

---

18c:23 • *the people* (*populum*), or perhaps "the apostle" (*apostolum*).

to come to meet the saint. ²When she came, she fell at his feet[a] and asked to hear the word of God.[b] ³Her request granted, she asked him to come to her estate, where a snake of astonishing size was devastating the entire region.

⁴As the apostle approached, the serpent hissed loudly, raised its head, and advanced to meet him. ⁵It was fifty cubits long, and everyone there was gripped by terror and fell to the ground.

⁶"Murderer!" said God's saint. "Hide the head you raised at the beginning for the destruction of humankind! ⁷Submit yourself to the servants of God—and die!"

⁸The snake immediately let out a deep roar, slithered around a mighty oak nearby, tied itself around it, vomited a stream of venom and blood, and perished.

⁹The holy apostle traveled to the woman's estate, where a young boy smitten by the snake lay dead. ¹⁰When Andrew saw his parents weeping he said to them, "Our God, who wants you to be saved, sent me here so that you may believe in him. Go now and see <for yourself> that your son's murderer is dead."

¹¹"We will not grieve our son's death," they said, "if we see revenge on his enemy."

¹²When they had left, the apostle said to the proconsul's wife, "Go and revive the boy."

¹³Without hesitation she went to the corpse and said, "Lad, in the name of my God Jesus Christ rise up unscathed." He got up at once.

¹⁴His parents returned jubilant at seeing the snake dead, and when they found their son alive they fell at the apostle's feet[a] and gave thanks.

20 The following night the blessed apostle saw a vision which he narrated to the other believers: ²"My good friends, listen to my dream. I saw a great mountain raised on high with nothing earthly on it, and it so radiated with light that it seemed to illumine the world. ³And there, standing with me, my beloved brothers, were

19:2 [a] → 3:3
[b] → 4:20

19:14 [a] → 3:3

19:5 • *fifty cubits*, that is, about eighty feet.
19:12 • *the proconsul's wife:* Gregory has said nothing earlier about Varianus's wife, presumably because the original story promoted radical asceticism as a condition of her conversion. This woman is probably Aristobula, who is mentioned, along with Maximilla of the *Acts of Andrew*, in *Man. Ps.* 143.13; 192.29.
20:1 • *to the . . . believers: fratribus*, presumably for τοῖς ἀδελφοῖς; see note on AcAndMt 3:3.

the apostles Peter and John. [4]Extending his hand to the apostle Peter, John raised him to the mountain's summit, turned, and asked me to go upward after Peter, saying, 'Andrew, you will drink Peter's cup.' [5]With his hands outstretched, he said, 'Come to me and stretch out your hands to join my hands, and let your head touch mine.' [6]When I did so, I discovered myself to be shorter than John. [7]'Would you like to know,' he then asked, 'to what this symbol you see refers, or who it is who speaks with you?'

[8]"'I long to know these things,' I said.

[9]"'I am the Word of the cross,'[a] he said, 'on which you soon will hang for the name of the One you proclaim.' [10]He also told me many other things about which I can say nothing now, but which will become apparent when I approach this sacrifice.[a] [11]For now, let all who have received the word of God[a] come together, and let me commend them to the Lord Jesus Christ, so that he may keep them untarnished in his teaching. [12]For I am already being untied from the body, and I go to that promise he saw fit to promise me—he who is Ruler of the heavens and earth, the Son of God Almighty, with the Holy Spirit, the true God enduring for ages everlasting." [13]When the believers[a] heard these things they wept uncontrollably, slapped their faces, and groaned.

[14]When everyone had arrived there, he said, "Beloved, I will be leaving you, but I trust in Jesus, whose word I preach, that he will keep you from evil, so that the enemy may not shred this harvest which I have tended among you, namely, the knowledge and teaching of Jesus Christ my Lord. [15]Therefore, pray continually and stand strong in the faith, so that the Lord may uproot every offensive weed and may consider you worthy of gathering into the heavenly granary as pure wheat."[a]

[16]In this manner he taught them and strengthened them in the commandments of God for five days. [17]After this, with hands outstretched, he prayed to the Lord: "O Lord, please guard this flock which already knows your salvation, so that the wicked one will not prevail, and that it may be entitled to guard forever unharmed what it received at your command and by my guidance."

[18]When he had said this, all present answered, "Amen!"

[19]He took the bread, gave thanks, broke it, and gave it to all, saying, "Receive the grace which Christ the Lord our God gives you

20:9 Cf. 1 Cor 1:18

20:10 [a]Cf. AAnPas 54

20:11 [a] → 4:20

20:13 [a] → AAnMt 3:3

20:15 [a]Cf. Mt 13:30

20:4 • *Peter's cup:* Andrew, too, will be crucified. Andrew's death and Peter's as recorded in the *Acts of Peter* have much in common, presumably the result of imitation in the *Acts of Andrew.* Cf. Mark 10:38–39; Matt 20:22–23; John 21:18–19.

through me his servant." [20]When he had kissed everyone and commended them to the Lord, he went on to Thessalonica. He taught there for two days and left them.

21

Many of the faithful from Macedonia went with him in two boats. [2]All of them sought to board the boat carrying the apostle, longing to hear him talk, so that not even while sailing would they be without the word of God.[a]

[3]The apostle said to them, "I know your desire, dear friends, but this boat is small. [4]Therefore, let the young men and baggage get aboard the larger ship, and you travel with us in this smaller one." [5]He gave them Anthimus to comfort them, and commanded them to board the other boat, which he ordered always to be nearby so that they, too, might see him and hear the word of God.[a]

[6]While he slept a little, someone was jarred by a moderate wind and fell into the sea.

[7]Anthimus woke him up, saying, "Good teacher, help! One of your servants is perishing!"

[8]The apostle awoke and rebuked the wind. It was silent and the sea once again became calm. [9]The person who had fallen in was carried to the ship with the help of a wave. Anthimus took his hand, lifted him on board, and all were amazed at the power of the apostle, for even the sea obeyed him.[a] [10]After twelve days, they landed at Patras, a city in Achaea; they disembarked, and stayed at some <nearby> residence.

21:2 [a] → 4:20

21:5 [a] → 4:20

21:9 Cf. Mk 4:41; Mt 8:27; Lk 8:25

Martyrium prius and the *Laudatio*, dependent on a common source, run parallel to Gregory for the next three chapters. Although generally these Greek recensions preserve the better readings, Gregory's account cannot be ruled out altogether. Here Lesbius claims that he had sent troops to the proconsul of Macedonia (Varianus?) to bring Andrew to Patras for execution, but the ship was lost at sea. *Martyrium prius* and *Laudatio* say nothing of this failed expedition, but one would hardly expect them to, since neither had mentioned Andrew's earlier problems with a proconsul in Macedonia. Therefore it is quite possible that such a back-reference in the ancient Acts, now preserved only by Gregory, was deleted from the Greek recensions to avoid confusion.

If this is the case, one might reconstruct Andrew's arrival like this: Patras is aswhirl with excitement and Lesbius orders the apostle to come before him. When Andrew arrives, he finds the proconsul nearly crazy with divine madness (so the *Martyrium prius* and *Laudatio*) or nearly dead from demonic thrashing (so Gregory). Lesbius tells the apostle about the shipwrecked mission to Macedonia (Gregory) and the cause of his sad predicament and asks for mercy. Andrew prays; the proconsul heals and converts. This reconstruction conflates the Latin and Greek traditions, neither of which conforms with it perfectly. But instead of offering a conjectural conflation of the two, what follows is a translation of the Greek with the Latin in the footnotes.

22 When he entered the city, a rumor spread that a stranger had entered the city— [2]reportedly naked, destitute, and bringing with him for his journey nothing but the name of a certain person named Jesus through whom he performs signs and great wonders, eradicates diseases, casts out demons, raises the dead, cures lepers, and heals every kind of suffering. [3]When the proconsul Lesbius heard this, he was disturbed and said, "He is a magician and charlatan! [4]We must not give him attention, but rather seek help from the gods." He wanted to arrest and destroy him.

[5]At night an angel of the Lord appeared to the proconsul Lesbius and with great fanfare and an awesome threat said, [6]"What have you suffered from this stranger Andrew such that you wickedly contrived to lay hands on him and cheated the God he preaches? [7]Now behold the hand of his Lord is on you, and you will be crazed until you know the truth through him." [8]The angel vanished from him, and he was struck dumb. [9]Not long after this, partially regaining his senses, he called his bodyguard and with tears said to them, "Take pity on me. [10]Quickly search the city for a certain stranger, a tramp called Andrew who preaches a foreign god through whom I will be able to learn the truth."[a] [11]They ardently sought out blessed Andrew, and when they found him, they brought him to the proconsul.

22:10 [a]AAnMt 24

22:1–4 GE "Later, when many people asked him to come to their homes, he said, 'As the Lord lives, I go nowhere unless my God commands it.' That night as he slept, he received no revelation. On the next night, as he was agonizing over this silence, he heard a voice saying to him, 'Andrew, I am with you always and will not leave you.' When he heard this, he glorified God for this vision."
22:4 GE "The proconsul Lesbius was warned in a vision to receive the man of God, and he sent for the person who receives and invites guests to bring the blessed apostle to him."
22:11 GE "When Andrew learned of the invitation, he went to the proconsul, entered his private chamber, and saw him lying prone, eyes closed, nearly dead. Poking his side, Andrew said, 'Get up and tell us what happened to you.'"

¹²Seeing him, the proconsul fell at his feet[a] and begged him: "Man of God, stranger and acquaintance of a strange god: ¹³take pity on one deceived, one estranged from the truth, one spotted with the stains of sins, one who knows many false gods but who is ignorant of the only true God. ¹⁴I beg the God in you, stretch out to me the hand of salvation, open to me the door of knowledge, shine on me the light of righteousness."

22:12 [a] → 3:3

¹⁵The blessed apostle, stunned and tearful at the words of the penitent, lifted up his eyes toward heaven, placed his right hand over his entire body, and said, ¹⁶"O my God Jesus Christ, unknown by the world but now revealed through us, you, Son of God, the Word, who was before all things and who pervades all things: ¹⁷Touch your servant and heal him, thereby bringing your vessel to completion, so that even he may be among your people, preaching your vigorous power." Immediately he grasped his right hand and raised him up.

¹⁸Getting up, he gave thanks to the Lord and said, "Stranger, surely he is God who needs neither hours nor days nor seasons. ¹⁹Therefore, I devote myself and my whole house[a] to you. I believe in the one who sent you to us."

22:19 [a] → 4:20

²⁰"Since you have believed so strongly in the one who sent me," Andrew told him, "you will be abundantly filled with knowledge."

²¹While matters were in this state, and while the entire city was rejoicing at the proconsul's salvation, crowds gathered from everywhere bringing those who were sick with various diseases. ²²He prayed for them, called on the Lord Jesus, laid his hands on them, and healed everyone. ²³Astonishment overtook all those living in the city, who shouted out, "Great is the power of the foreign God! Great is the God preached by the stranger Andrew. ²⁴From today on let's destroy the statues of our idols, let's cut down their groves, let's crush their monuments, let's reject the polytheistic knowledge of vain demons. ²⁵Let's recognize rather the only God, the one preached by Andrew. Great is the God of Andrew!"

22:14 GE "I am the one who cursed the Way which you teach," he said, "and I sent soldiers and ships to the proconsul of Macedonia to send you to me bound, so that I might condemn you to death. But they suffered shipwreck and were unable to get where they had been commanded to go. Because I persisted in my intention to destroy your Way, two Ethiopians [i.e., demons] appeared to me, beat me with whips, and said, 'We are no longer able to exercise power here, because that man you planned to persecute is on his way. And now, this very night, while we still have power, we will avenge ourselves on you.' I was thus severely beaten and they left me. Now, O man of God, pray to the Lord, so that by his forgiving me this crime I may be cured of my infirmity."

22:20 GE "When he had narrated this to all the people, the blessed apostle preached the word of God continually [see 4:20], and all believed. The proconsul was healed, believed, and was strengthened in the faith."

²⁶Together they all rushed to the temples and burned up, pulverized, cut down, scorned, trampled on, and destroyed their gods, saying, "Let Andrew's God alone be named!"

²⁷The proconsul Lesbius likewise rejoiced at the cry of the citizenry and exulted at the action of the crowd.

23 Then Trophime, at one time the proconsul's mistress and currently the lover of yet another man, left her husband and devoted herself to apostolic teaching. ²For this purpose she often visited the house of the proconsul where the apostle constantly taught. ³Her enraged husband came to her lady and said, "Trophime is resuming her former prostitution with my lord the proconsul, and now once again sleeps with him."

⁴Ablaze with bitterness, she said, "So that's why my husband deserted me and for the last six months has not made love with me: he prefers his maidservant!" ⁵She called for the steward and ordered Trophime condemned to prostitution. Without delay she was led away to a brothel and given to a pimp. ⁶Lesbius knew nothing of these developments, and when he inquired about Trophime, his wife lied to him <about it>.

⁷Trophime entered the brothel and prayed incessantly. Whenever men came to touch her, she would place on her breast the Gospel that she had with her, and all the men would pull back and not approach her. ⁸A particularly shameless rogue came to violate her, and when she resisted, he tore off her clothes, and the Gospel fell to the ground. ⁹Trophime cried, stretched her hands toward heaven, and said, "Don't let me be defiled, O Lord, for whose name I value chastity!"

¹⁰Immediately an angel of the Lord appeared to the young man, and he fell at the angel's feet and died. ¹¹When she had been comforted, she blessed and glorified the Lord, who had not allowed her to be abused. ¹²Later she raised the lad in the name of Jesus Christ, and the whole city ran to <see> the sight.

¹³The wife of the proconsul went off to the bath with her pimp. While they were washing together, a hideous demon appeared to them and beat them both so severely that they fell and died. ¹⁴There was great wailing, and the report came to the apostle and to the proconsul that Lesbius's wife and the pimp were dead.

¹⁵When blessed Andrew heard this news, he said to the people, "Dear friends, see how the enemy prevails, for they condemned

---

23:3 • *her lady*, i.e., Lesbius's wife.
23:15 • *<her> chastity*, or possibly "*<his> chastity*," i.e., Lesbius's.

Trophime to prostitution on account of <her> chastity. [16]But now God's judgment has arrived: Look, the pimp and the lady of the house who ordered Trophime put in a brothel have been battered to death in the bath."

[17]When he had said this, the lady's nurse arrived, who because of old age was carried about in the arms of others, her clothing ripped, crying loudly. [18]She was placed before the apostle and began to beg him, "We know that you are beloved of God, and that whatever you ask your God he accomplishes for you.[a] Now have mercy on me and raise her."

23:18 Cf. Mk 11:24; Mt 21:22; Jn 14:13–14

[19]The blessed apostle, moved by the woman's tears, turned to the proconsul and said, "Do you want her revived?"

[20]"Let her not live," he said, "for having committed such a scandal in my house."

[21]"Don't act like that," said the apostle, "for we should show mercy to those seeking it, so that we may obtain mercy from God."[a]

23:21 [a]Cf. Mt 18:33; Jas 2:13

[22]When Andrew had said this, the proconsul went to the praetorium, and the holy apostle ordered the body displayed before everyone. [23]He approached the body and said, "Kind Lord Jesus Christ, I ask that this woman be revived, and that all may know that you are the Lord God, who alone is merciful and just, who does not allow the innocent to perish." [24]He turned around, touched the head of the woman and said, "Rise up in the name of Jesus Christ, my God."

[25]Immediately the woman rose up, wept, moaned, hung her head, and looked at the ground. [26]"Go to your room," the apostle told her, "and pray in secret until you are comforted by the Lord."

[27]"Let me first make peace with Trophime," she replied, "on whom I have brought so much harm."

[28]"Have no fear," said the holy apostle. "Trophime does not hold these wicked acts against you nor does she seek revenge, but gives thanks to God for whatever happens to her." [29]When Trophime was

---

23:29 • Apparently the raising of Callisto had been narrated earlier but was passed over by Gregory.

23:32 M 7 (=L 36) "Because a great crowd was causing a disturbance, and because the word of blessed Andrew and his preaching spread everywhere unresisted, the emperor sent a successor for Lesbius and terminated his rule. On receiving the imperial decree, Lesbius went with joy to blessed Andrew and said, 'Now I will believe in the Lord even more, because I have shed vain glory, put off the pride of the world, and thrown aside the distraction of life. Therefore, man of God, take me as your fellow traveler. Receive me as a devotee who speaks faithfully and witnesses to all people concerning our common Savior, Christ.' Leaving the praetorium, he traveled with Andrew"; L adds "touring all the territory of Achaea with the announcer of the divine preaching."

summoned, he reconciled her with Callisto, the proconsul's wife, who had been raised.

³⁰Lesbius so progressed in the faith that one day he came to the apostle to confess all his sins. ³¹The holy apostle told him, "I thank God, my son, that you fear the coming judgment. Be of courage and strong in the Lord in whom you believe." ³²He took his hand and walked with him on the seashore.

24 After the walk, while he was seated, other individuals too would sit with him on the sand hearing the word of God,ᵃ when a corpse that had rotted in the sea was thrown onto the shore at the apostle's feet. ²Then the holy apostle rejoiced in the Lord and said, "This corpse should be resuscitated, so that we may learn what the enemy has done to him." ³After he had spoken a prayer, he grabbed the dead man's hand, lifted him up, and immediately he came to life and began to speak. ⁴Because the man was nude, Andrew gave him a tunic; and <then> he said, "Explain to us in detail all that happened to you."

⁵"I will hide nothing from you, whoever you are," he said. "I am the son of Sostratus, a citizen of Macedonia, recently arrived from Italy. ⁶When I returned home I heard that a new teachingᵃ had arisen which no one had ever heard before, and that a certain teacher who asserts that he is a disciple of the true God performs signs, portents, and wondrous cures. ⁷When I heard these things I hurried to see him, because I decided only this: that it was God himself who was doing such things. ⁸While I was sailing with my slaves and friends, a storm suddenly broke out, the sea went wild, and we were overcome by the turbulence. ⁹If only we had been thrown up on shore together, so that the others too might have been revived by you as I was!"

¹⁰When he had said these things, he turned many things over in his mind and decided that this person was the apostle whom he had sought. ¹¹He fell at his feetᵃ and said, "I know that you are a servant of the true God. ¹²I beg you for those who were with me, that they too may regain life with your help, so that they may know the true God whom you preach."

¹³Then the holy apostle, full of the Holy Spirit,ᵃ continuously preached to him the word of God,ᵇ so that the boy marveled at his teaching. ¹⁴Then he put his hands up and said, "O Lord, I ask that you bring forth the rest of the corpses, that they too may know that you are the true and only God."

¹⁵After he had said this, immediately thirty-nine corpses appeared on the shore, washed up by a cooperative wave. ¹⁶At the

24:1 ᵃ → 4:20

24:6 ᵃCf. Mk 1:27

24:11 ᵃ → 3:3

24:13 ᵃCf. Ac 4:8
ᵇ → 4:20

24:16 ᵃ → 3:3

youth's weeping, everyone else began to weep, and falling at the apostle's feet[a] they asked that these too be revived. [17]For his part, Philopater (this was the lad's name)[a] said, "With good intentions my father laded the ship with my necessities and sent me here with a lot of money. [18]But now if he hears what has happened to me, he might blaspheme your God and suppress his teaching. May it not be so!"

24:17[a] → 13:6

[19]As everyone wept, the apostle asked that the bodies be collected, for they had been scattered about. [20]When all had been brought together, the apostle said, "Whom do you wish raised first?"

[21]"Varus," he said, "my foster brother."

[22]Then Andrew knelt to the ground, raised the palms of his hands to heaven, and prayed for a long time, crying: [23]"Good Jesus, raise this dead man who was reared with Philopater, that he may know your glory and that your name may be magnified among the people."

[24]Immediately the boy got up, and everyone there was astonished.

[25]The apostle again poured out prayer for each one of the others, saying, "Lord Jesus, I ask that these who have been swept here from the depths of the sea also may rise again." [26]Then he ordered each of the brothers to take a corpse and say, "Jesus Christ, the Son of the living God, revives you." [27]When this was done, the thirty-eight were raised up, and the spectators glorified God: "None is like you, O Lord." [28]Lesbius gave Philopater many gifts, saying, "Don't let this economic loss sadden you, and don't depart from the servant of God." [29]So he was continuously with the apostle, attentive to everything he said.

25

There was a woman named Calliope who had slept with a murderer and conceived a child out of wedlock. [2]When the time for her delivery came, she had hard labor and was not able to deliver. [3]She said to her sister, "Please go and invoke our goddess Diana to take pity on me, for she is the deity of childbearing."

[4]When her sister did as she had been ordered, the devil came to her at night and said, "Why do you uselessly invoke me, since I am unable to help you? [5]Go instead to Andrew the apostle of God, in Achaea, and he will take pity on your sister."

[6]So the woman got up and went to the apostle and told him everything. [7]Without delay, he went to Corinth to the house of the

25:3 • *Diana*, i.e., the Greek goddess Artemis.

suffering woman; Lesbius the proconsul was with him. [8]When the blessed apostle saw the woman writhing from the tortures of <her> hard labor, he said, "It's quite fitting that you suffer these pains! [9]You endure intolerable torments because you married badly and conceived with a trickster; not only that, you consulted demons who cannot help anyone, not even themselves. [10]Now believe in Jesus Christ, the Son of God, and bring forth your infant, but the baby will be stillborn because you conceived it unworthily." [11]The woman believed, and when everyone had left the room, she gave birth to a dead baby. And so it was that was she relieved of her suffering.

26 When the blessed apostle had done many signs and portents in Corinth, Sostratus, Philopater's father, was warned in a vision to visit the apostle. [2]He went to Achaea, but when he did not find him, he went on to Corinth. [3]As Andrew was walking with Lesbius and others, Sostratus recognized him, for he looked just as he had in the dream. [4]Embracing his feet he said, "Please have pity on me, servant of God, as you had pity on my son."

[5]Philopater told the apostle: "This man you see is my father. He now asks what he should do."

[6]"I know," said the blessed apostle. "He comes to us so as to know the truth. We thank our Lord Jesus Christ, who deigns to reveal himself to those who believe."

[7]Sostratus's slave Leontius said to him, "Master, do you see how the man's face shines with light?"[a]

[8]"I do see, dear friend," said Sostratus. "And for that reason we should not separate from him, but let us live together with him and hear the words of eternal life."[a]

[9]On the next day, he offered the apostle many gifts, but God's saint told him, "I cannot accept anything from you, but I would make you yourselves my prize by your believing in Jesus who sent me to evangelize in this place. [10]Had I desired money, I would have prevailed on the more opulent Lesbius, who could make me exceedingly wealthy. Offer me instead whatever promotes your salvation."

27 A few days later he ordered a bath prepared for him, and when he went there to bathe he saw an old man possessed by a demon, trembling terribly. [2]As he wondered at him, a young boy

26:7 [a] → 11:15

26:8 [a]Cf. Jn 6:68

27:2 [a] → 3:3
[b]Cf. 17:7; Mk 1:24; 5:7; Mt 8:29; Lk 4:34; 8:28

25:11 • *a dead baby:* There is a possible biblical precedent to this judgment in the death of the first child of David and Bathsheba (2 Sam 12:14, 18–19).

came from the pool, fell at the apostle's feet,[a] and said, "What do we have to do with you, Andrew? Have you come here to tear us from our dwellings?"[b]

[3]The apostle got up and said to the bystanders, "Don't be afraid, but believe in Jesus our Savior."[a]

[4]"We believe what you preach," they all cried.

[5]He rebuked each demon, and they deserted the bodies they haunted. [6]The old man and the youth were given permission to return to their own homes.[a]

[7]As the blessed apostle bathed, he spoke as follows: "The enemy of humankind[a] lies in ambush everywhere, whether in baths or in rivers. [8]For that reason we must constantly invoke the name of the Lord, so that he who wants to ambush you will have no power."

[9]When the men of the city saw this, they left, brought back the sick and placed them before him: <and> they were <all> healed. [10]People also came from other cities bringing the sick, and these too were healed and gladly heard the word of God.[a]

28 While this was going on, an old man named Nicolaus came to the apostle wearing torn clothing and saying, [2]"Servant of God, I have lived for seventy-four years, and during this time I persisted in debauchery, prostitution, and fornication; often I ran impulsively to the brothel and engaged in illicit sex. [3]But two days ago I heard of the miracles you do, and your speeches, which are full of life-giving words. [4]I thought to myself that I would abandon my debauchery and come to you, so that you might show me a better way of life. [5]But while I considered this, another feeling came over me, namely, that I should abandon and not do the good I had intended. [6]Then, in a struggle of conscience, I took a Gospel and prayed to the Lord to make me forget these things once and for all. [7]A few days later, when my perverse thoughts were inflamed, I went again to a brothel unaware of the Gospel I had with me. [8]A whore saw me and said, 'Get away, get away, old man, for you are an angel of God! Don't touch me or come near here—I see in you a great mystery.' [9]Stupefied, I considered what this mystery might be; and <then> I remembered that I had a Gospel with me. [10]I spun around and came to you, servant of God, so that you may have pity on my vices. [11]I have the greatest hope that I will not perish if you pray for my wretchedness."

[12]When blessed Andrew heard this, he spoke at length against fornication; <then> he knelt, stretched out his hands, prayed silently, uttered groans, and wept from the sixth hour to the ninth. [13]Then he got up, washed his face, and desired to eat nothing: "I

27:3 [a]Cf. Mk 5:36; Lk 8:50

27:6 [a]Cf. Mk 5:19; Lk 8:39

27:7 [a] → 5:5

27:10 [a] → 4:20

will not eat until I know if God will take pity on this man, and if he should be counted among the saved." [14]He fasted the next day as well, but nothing was revealed to him about this man until the fifth day, on which he cried uncontrollably and said, "Lord, we obtain your mercy for the dead, so why is this man who desires to know your marvelous deeds not able to reform, so that you may heal him?"

28:15 [a] → AAnMt 3:1

[15]When he had said this, a voice came down from heaven, saying,[a] "Andrew, you have obtained your request for this old man. But for him to be saved, he must fast until he is exhausted, just as you did." [16]Andrew called the old man and preached abstinence.

28:17 [a] → APaTh 23:7

[17]On the sixth day,[a] he summoned his followers and asked them all to pray for Nicolaus. [18]They prostrated themselves on the ground and prayed: "Kind, compassionate Lord, forgive this man's offense." [19]Once this was done, Andrew ate a little bit and allowed the others to eat.

[20]Nicolaus returned home and gave all his possessions to the poor. He so tortured himself that for six months he drank only water and ate only dry bread. [21]And so, having performed the proper penance, he passed from this world. [22]The blessed apostle was not present, but a voice came to him where he was, saying, "Andrew,

28:23 [a] → AAnMt 3:3

Nicolaus, for whom you interceded, has become mine." [23]He gave thanks, told the believers[a] that Nicolaus had departed from the body, and prayed that he might rest in peace.

29 When he was staying at that place, Antiphanes, a citizen of Megara, came to him and said, [2]"Blessed Andrew, if you have any of the kindness commanded by the Savior whom you preach, show it now and free my house from the calamity threatening it, for it is in terrible turmoil."

[3]"Tell us, sir, what's happened to you," said the apostle.

[4]"When I returned home from a journey," he said, "I passed through the entrance to my atrium and heard the voice of my porter crying miserably. [5]When I asked why, those present told me that he was severely tortured by a demon, along with his wife and son. [6]When I went upstairs, I saw other servants grinding their teeth, attacking me, and laughing hysterically. [7]I went past them up to the top floor where my wife was lying, having been badly battered by them. [8]She was so disturbed, so weary with madness, <her> hair

---

29:1 • *that place,* i.e., Sparta.
29:6 • *laughing hysterically* (*adridentes risos insanos*): See notes on 6:13; AcPaulThec 4:1; and esp. AcPetVerc 11:2 (demonically inspired laughter).

falling in front of her eyes, that she couldn't see or recognize me. [9]Her alone I ask you to restore to me; I'm not concerned about the others."

[10]Then, moved with compassion, the holy apostle said, "There is no respect of persons with God,[a] who came to save all the lost.[b] So then," he said, "let's go to his house."

[11]He left Lacedaemon, came to Megara, and went through the entrance to the house. [12]Immediately all the demons cried out with the fury of a single voice: "Holy Andrew, why do you persecute us here? Why are you in a house not given to you? [13]Occupy those houses which are yours, but don't in addition infiltrate those given to us!"

[14]The holy apostle was astonished at them and went upstairs to the bedroom where the woman lay. [15]When he had prayed, he took her hand and said, "May the Lord Jesus Christ heal you."[a] Immediately the woman got up from the bed and blessed God. [16]In the same way he laid hands on each one who had been harassed by a demon, restored them to health, and accepted Antiphanes and his wife as wonderfully strong associates in preaching the word of God.[a]

[17]Blessed Andrew then saw a vision: it seemed that the Savior, Christ, stood before him telling him, "Andrew, place the Spirit on Lesbius and give him your grace. [18]Take up your cross and follow me,[a] because tomorrow I will cast you from the world. Hurry on to Patras." [19]On waking, the apostle disclosed to those with him the seeing of the vision, and he waited for the completion of this <divine> word.

30
Andrew and his disciples entered <Patras>, and a man named Sosius, whom Andrew had healed of a terminal illness, received them. [2]As he walked about the city, he saw a paralytic thrown down on a dungheap. [3]Andrew went up to him, gave him his hand, and raised him up by calling on Christ.

Marginal references:

29:10 [a]Cf. Ac 10:34; Rm 2:11; Gal 2:6; Eph 6:9; Col 3:25
[b]Cf. Mt 18:11; Lk 19:10

29:15 [a]Cf. Ac 9:34

29:16 [a] → 4:20

29:18 [a]Cf. Mk 8:34; Mt 16:24; 10:38; Lk 9:23; 14:27

29:17 • *Blessed Andrew . . .:* The following passage does not appear in Gregory; one cannot be certain that it ever appeared in the ancient *Acts of Andrew*.
29:18 • *tomorrow:* αὔριον, or possibly τάχιον ("soon"), with L.

29:19 M continues "Then someone burst in upon the apostle and said, 'The emperor sent Aegeates to administer the proconsulship, and wicked slaves of the devil, enemies of humankind [cf. 5:5], have introduced him into the regions of Achaea'"; L "Doing as he had been ordered, he arrives in Patras that very day."

30:3 GE "Then the blessed apostle came to the city of Patras, where Aegeates was proconsul, having recently succeeded Lesbius." GE 30–32 has parallels in M and L. The translation that follows is based on an eclectic text; words in italics come from Gregory's Latin.

30:5 ª → 4:20

30:6 ª → 3:3

30:7 ªCf. 33:3; Mk 5:26; Lk 8:43

30:12 ªCf. Ac 16:28
ᵇCf. Mt 26:52

30:15 ªCf. Mk 1:31; Mt 8:15; Lk 4:39
ᵇCf. Mk 5:43

30:18 ªCf. Mt 10:8

⁴As reports of the healing circulated, Maximilla, the proconsul's wife, sent her faithful servant Iphidama as someone she trusted as her representative—someone who might speak with and hear Andrew. ⁵When Iphidama left she met Sosius, Andrew's disciple, who warmly welcomed her and instructed her in the word of Godª and in divine healing. ⁶When he brought her to Andrew she fell at his feetª and listened to his words. Then she told her mistress <what had happened>.

⁷A few days later, Maximilla, the proconsul's wife, took sick. Despairing of physicians, who had proven useless,ª she sent Iphidama and summoned Andrew. ⁸*"Holy Andrew," Iphidama said, "my mistress Maximilla, who is suffering from a high fever, asks you to come to her, for she strongly desires to hear your teaching. ⁹Her husband the proconsul stands at the bed crying and wielding a sword in his hand, so that when she expires he can stab himself with the blade."*

¹⁰He and his disciples went with her and entered *the bedroom where the unfortunate woman lay.* ¹¹He found the proconsul clasping a sword and awaiting his wife's demise, wishing to do away with himself so as to die with her. ¹²Andrew spoke to him softly: "Do yourself no harm.ª Put your sword back in its scabbard,ᵇ child, *for a time will come when it will be drawn against us."*

¹³*Though the ruler understood nothing of this, he allowed him to go on his way.*

¹⁴*The apostle then went to the sick woman's cot* and rebuked the fever, saying, "Fever, leave her alone!" ¹⁵He put his hands on her: right away she broke into a sweat, *and the fever left her;*ª a little later she wanted something to eat.ᵇ ¹⁷Aegeates offered him *one hundred silver coins* and said, "Take your pay."

¹⁸Andrew refused to take anything, saying, "We have received freely, so we freely give.ª But offer yourself to God—if you can!"

31 Leaving there, the blessed one, weary with old age, was propped up by his own disciples, and he saw someone who had been paralyzed for a long time lying inside the portico, begging. ²*Many of the citizens used to give him a pittance for his food.* ³Andrew

---

30:15 *E* continues "and immediately she arose. Many who saw this believed. But Aegeates, being Greek, mistook Andrew for a doctor, and was unwilling to hear the word of God" (see 4:20); *L* "Having been strengthened beyond expectation, she rose up and glorified God. Many of those who saw the incredible healing believed on the Lord, but the proconsul, beguiled by Greek errors, would not allow himself to hear the divine oracles."

30:18 *We have received . . . if you can:* So *E; L* "'Retain this reward, for you are worth it! My reward will come to me quickly'—by which he meant Maximilla" (cf. Isa 40:10; 62:11; Rev 2:16; 3:11; 22:7, 12, 20).

said to him, "Jesus the Christ heals you!" He gave him his hand, and at once the man became well. [4]He ran through the middle of the city showing himself off and glorifying God.

32 As he went on from there, he saw a man with his wife and son, all blind, *and he said, "Truly this is the work of the devil, for he has blinded them in mind and body.* [2]*To them he said, "In the name of my God, Jesus Christ, I restore to you the light of your physical eyes.* [3]*He also deigns to unlock the darkness of your minds, so that you may be saved by recognizing the light which illumines everyone who comes into this world."*[a] [4]He touched their eyes, and immediately they received their sight and kissed his feet, glorifying and thanking God. [5]When the crowd saw this, they were struck with astonishment, and many believed.

33 Some people came to him and asked him not to recoil from going also to the harbor, for they said that there, thrown on a dung-heap, was a certain man, one of the ancients, of noble pedigree and renown, who had become shriveled and hideous with leprosy and who reeked with stench: [2]"Passers-by throw scraps to him as to a dog, not daring to approach anyone so utterly ulcerated. [3]Time and again all of Patras has offered to give handsome sums to various physicians to heal him, because he was the son of one of their celebrated fleet commanders; but he was unable to get even the slightest relief from any of them."[a]

[4]When Andrew heard this, he was moved to compassion[a] and went to him. [5]Many of those in the crowd went with him, inquisitive about what would happen, but because no one else could tolerate the efflux of stench only Andrew approached the man. [6]"I have come to you," Andrew told him, "so that I may heal you through my physician."

[7]"Friend," he said, "is your physician divine or human? No human can heal me."

[8]"I detect that you are truly being saved," Andrew told him, "for even now God is present with you to raise you up from here, for I have called to him with visible sounds. [9]You will see in yourself the power of the sounds, for you will walk with me—healed!"

[10]When he had said this to the sick man, who was shocked by Andrew's promise, the apostle prayed, and after praying he stripped the invalid of all the rags he was wearing—putrid and

32:3 [a]Cf. Jn 1:9

33:3 [a] → 30:7

33:4 [a]Cf. Mk 1:41; 6:34; 8:2; Mt 9:36; 14:14; 15:32; 18:27; 20:24; Lk 7:13; 10:33; 15:20

32:5 GE "and they said, 'There is no other God but the one whom his servant Andrew preaches.'"

33:2 *so utterly ulcerated:* E adds "When they bring him food, they hold their noses and leave quickly."

dripping with pus from the old man's many revolting sores. [11]As the rags dropped to the earth, many maggots filled the spot. [12]There was a short distance between the ground where he was lying and the sea, and Andrew commanded him to get up and walk with him. [13]By the Lord's power, he stood up without any assistance and went off with the apostle, as large quantities of pus dripped from him—in fact, as his entire body oozed. [14]So abundant was the flow of pus that wherever he walked there was a trail of moisture clearly visible to everyone.

[15]When they both got to the sea, the apostle spoke to him again: "Now I wash your body so that it may be made well. You yourself will wash your soul." [16]He lifted him up, brought him to the sea, and brought him out. By the Lord's grace, the man immediately became whole, without a blemish on his body—no ulcer, no wound, no scar—but was vibrant and had a pure body. [17]Everyone who saw him was amazed and glorified God with loud voices at the beach, with the result that the proconsul heard right away what had happened.

[18]Just when the apostle commanded him to be given clothes, the one who earlier had been neglected and weak was now so transported by joy that he did not want to take them but ran through the city naked and screaming, so that his prior acquaintances could contrast what they had known him to be with what he had <now> become. [19]He went to their city square and shouted, "I thank you, O God who sent your man to me! I thank you, you who had mercy on me! [20]Everyone had given up hope for me, but you alone showed compassion. No one dared to draw near to me, but now all draw near to your glory."

[21]As he was speaking many such things, stark naked, he still hesitated taking up his <new> clothing until the apostle arrived and ordered him to get dressed. [22]When he had taken the garments and dressed himself, he followed the apostle. [23]Everyone saw that he had become well, and they were astounded.

THE PASSION OF ANDREW

1 At the same time that his wife was healed, the proconsul Aegeates took leave for Rome, to the emperor Nero. ²Stratocles, Aegeates's brother, who had petitioned Caesar not to serve in the army but to pursue philosophy, arrived in Patras from Italy at that very moment. ³Excitement overtook the entire praetorium of Aristocles, because Stratocles had not come to visit Aegeates for a long time. ⁴Maximilla too left the bedroom, delighted to greet him, and when she had welcomed Stratocles, she went in with him. ⁵At daybreak, she was alone while Stratocles fulfilled his duty to his friends—gently mingling with everyone there and greeting them all graciously and with decorum.

2 As he (Stratocles) was engaged in this way, one of the boys under the leadership of Aristocles was stricken by a demon and lay in feces, out of his mind. ²When Stratocles saw him he said, "If only I had never come here but had perished at sea this would not have happened to me! Friends," glancing at those with him, "I cannot live without him." ³As he said this, he hit himself about the eyes and became deeply distressed and unwilling to be looked at <by anyone>. He was at a loss as to what to do.

⁴When Maximilla heard about this, she too emerged upset from her bedroom and said to Stratocles, "Don't worry about your servant, brother. ⁵Soon he will be healed, for there is a most God-fearing man staying in this city who not only can dispel demons, but, if some menacing and serious sickness overcomes someone, he cures it. ⁶We have come to trust in him, but we say this as those who have put him to the test." ⁷Iphidama likewise said such things to Stratocles, to restrain him from venturing some rash act—he was so altogether distraught.

1:3 • *of Aristocles*, or "on account of Stratocles" (Prieur).

2:1 *Aristocles* or "Stratocles" (Prieur); *L* adds "who had been talked into serving with the most trust-worthy, whom Stratocles loved dearly, Alcmàn by name"; *HS* "whom he loved dearly."

3 While both women were consoling Stratocles, Andrew, having agreed with Maximilla that he would go to the boy, arrived at the praetorium. ²On entering the gate he said, "Some force is fighting inside; hurry, brothers!" ³He asked questions of no one but burst inside, to the place where Stratocles's lad was foaming at the mouth, entirely twisted about.

⁴Those who came dashing in because of Stratocles's ruckus had no idea who Andrew was when they saw him smiling and shoving aside those who were present, making a path <through the crowd> in order to get to the lad lying on the ground. ⁵Those who had already met Andrew and had seen him at work <readily> gave ground, fearing him like some god. ⁶Stratocles's servants, on the other hand, viewed him as a shabby tramp and tried to beat him up. ⁷When the rest saw them maltreating him, they rebuked them for not knowing what they were doing. When they settled down, they waited to see what would happen.

4 Just then someone told Maximilla and Iphidama that the blessed one had arrived. ²They were elated, sped from their rooms, and hurried to Stratocles: "Come and you will see how your servant is healed."

³Stratocles too got up and walked with them, and when he saw the enormous crowd standing around his servant, he said quietly,

4:4 ᵃ → AAnGE 13:6

⁴"Alcman" (this was the boy's name),ᵃ "you have become a spectacle by coming to Achaea!"

⁵Andrew stared at Maximilla, and while looking at her he said the following: "My child, this is what is most distressing to those who are turning to a faith in God away from a great tempest and wandering: to see these ailments cured which many considered beyond help. ⁶Look, even now I see what I am saying coming to pass: magicians are standing here helpless to do anything—those who had given up on the lad, and others we all see huckstering in public.

4:7 ᵃCf. Mk 3:23–26; Mt 12:25–26; Lk 11:17–18

⁷Why have they been unable to expel this fearsome demon from the pitiful lad? Because they are kindred to it.ᵃ ⁸It is useful to say this before the present crowd."

5 Without delay he got up and said, "O God who does not give heed to magicians, O God who does not offer yourself to the quacks, ²O God who withdraws from things foreign (to yourself), O God who always offers your possessions to your own— ³even now, in the

---

3:4 • *smiling* (μειδιῶντα): See note on AcAndGE 16:3.

presence of all these people, grant my request quickly with respect to Stratocles's servant by banishing the demon whom those who are its kindred could not."

⁴Immediately the demon relented and said in a masculine voice, "I flee, servant of God! I flee not only from this lad but also from this entire city."

⁵"I not only command you to flee from this city," Andrew told him. "I bar you from setting foot in any of those regions where there is so much as a trace of my brothers and sisters."ᵃ

⁶When the demon had left, Alcman got up from the ground: then Andrew extended his hand to him, and the lad walked with him, self-composed, steady on his feet, conducting coherent conversation, affectionately looking at Andrew and his master, and inquiring about the reason for the crowd inside.ᵃ ⁷Andrew told him, "There is no need for you to learn anything alien to you. It is enough for us to see in you what we have seen."

6 While they were occupied with those things, Maximilla took Andrew and Stratocles by the hand and went into her bedroom along with those of the believersᵃ who were there. ²Once seated, they fixed their eyes on blessed Andrew, to hear him speak. ³For the sake of Stratocles, Maximilla had been eager for the apostle to talk so that he might believe in the Lord. ⁴His brother Aegeates was in every respect blasphemous—despicable in his indifference to good or bad.

7 "O Stratocles," Andrew began, "I know well that you are moved by what has happened, but I am also certain that I must bring out into the open the person now latent within you. ²Your complete bewilderment and pondering of the source and cause of what has happened are the greatest proofs that the soul within you is troubled, and the perplexity, hesitation, and astonishment in you please me. ³Bring to birth the child you are carrying and do not give yourself over to labor pains alone. ⁴I am no novice at midwifery or divination. I desire what you are birthing. I love what you are <presently> stifling. I will suckle what is within you. I know the one who is silent. I know the one who aspires. ⁵Already your new self speaks to me. Already I encounter those things he has suffered for so long. ⁶He is ashamed of his former religion; he mourns his former public conduct; he considers all his former worship vacuous; he has no idea what true religion is; ⁷he tacitly reproaches the useless gods

5:5 ᵃ → AAnMt 3:3

5:6 ᵃCf. 10:3

6:1 ᵃ → AAnMt 3:3

of his past; having become a vagabond, he suffers in order to become educated. [8]Whatever his former philosophy, he now knows that it was hollow. He sees that it is destitute and worthless. [9]Now he learns that it promises nothing essential. Now he admits that it pledges nothing useful. [10]Right? Doesn't the person inside you say these things, Stratocles?"

8 After a loud groan, Stratocles answered as follows: "Most prophetic man, truly a messenger of the living God, I too will not separate from you until I recognize myself by having despised all those things for which you rebuked me for idly squandering my time in them."

8:2 [a]Cf. 10:4; 13:1; 23:7; → APaTh 7:1

[2]Stratocles was with the apostle night and day[a] and never left him: sometimes examining, learning from, and interrupting him, at other times silent and enjoying himself, having truly become enamored of saving attentiveness. [3]Declaring that he would bid adieu to all his possessions, he decided to live alone, with no one else but the apostle. [4]He ceased altogether examining the blessed one when anyone else was present, but while the rest of the believers were doing something else, he questioned him in private. [5]When the others fell asleep, he would lie awake and by his enthusiastic interruptions would not let Andrew sleep.

9:1 [a] → AAnMt 3:3

9 Andrew would not keep quiet but exposed Stratocles's inquiries to the believers[a] by telling him, "Stratocles, double your harvest by asking me questions in private and by hearing the same in the presence of the brothers and sisters here. [2]That way, what you desire and seek will all the more surely be stored up in you; it's not right for you to hide your labor pains even from your peers. [3]Take the example of a woman in labor: when the labor pains overcome her and the fetus is pushed by some power to come forth—not to stay within but to be squeezed outside—the fetus becomes obvious and noticeable to the attending women who take part in such mysteries (it was the fetus itself that cried out when the mother cried out earlier). [4]Then, after she has given birth, these initiates at last provide for the newborn whatever care they know, so that, so far as it's up to them, the fetus can be born alive. [5]Likewise, Stratocles my child, we too must not be passive but bring your embryos into the open, so that they may be registered and be brought to the gift of

---

8:1 • *messenger*, or "angel" (ἄγγελος).

saving words by many brothers and sisters, whose associate I find you to be."

10 Maximilla and Iphidama were overjoyed that Stratocles was conducting himself in a pious manner— [2]at last he was firmly established on all the words that were part of his true nature, and <at last> he possessed a steady soul and a firm and unalterable faith in the Lord. [3]Alcman, already cured,[a] no longer resisted the faith. [4]Because they were rejoicing and being confirmed in Christ night and day,[a] Stratocles, full of gratitude, and Maximilla, Iphidama, Alcman, along with many of the other believers[b]—<all of them> were deemed worthy of the Lord's seal.

11 "My children," Andrew told them, "if you keep this seal's impression unconfused with other seals that imprint different designs, God will commend you and receive you into his domain. [2]A radiant image appears in your souls, set loose from your bodies; [3]so that the punishing powers—evil authorities, fearsome rulers, fiery angels, hideous demons, and foul forces, who cannot endure being forsaken by you, and are alien to the symbol of the seal since it is kindred to light— [4]<these forces, all of them,> run aground and sink during their flight to their kindred: darkness, fire, gloom, and whatever other impending punishment one might imagine. [5]But if you pollute the brilliance of the grace given you, those awful powers will taunt you and toy with you by dancing here and there: like an impostor or a tyrant, each will demand its own. [6]Then it will do you no good to call on the God of your seal which you defiled by apostatizing from him.

12 "So, my children, let us guard the deposit entrusted to us: let us return the deposit spotless to the one who entrusted it to us. [2]When we arrive there, let's say to him, 'Look, we brought you your gift unabused. Which of your possessions will you give us?' [3]He will answer us at once, 'I will give you myself. All that I am I give to my own: [4]If you desire unflickering light, I am it. If you desire a life not subject to coming-to-be, I am it. [5]If you desire rest from futile

10:3 [a]Cf. 5:6
10:4 [a] → 8:2
         [b] → AAnMt 3:3

12:5 [a]Cf. Mt 11:28

12:1 • *guard the deposit entrusted to us:* φυλάξωμεν . . . τὴν πιστευθεῖσαν ἡμῖν παρακαταθήκην; cf. AAnGE 6:12; 1 Tim 6:20 τὴν παρακαταθήκην [TR παρακαταθήκην] φύλαξον (also 2 Tim 1:12, 14); 2 Thess 2:15 "hold fast to the traditions that you were taught (κρατεῖτε τὰς παραδόσεις)"; *Did.* 4.13 "Keep what you received (φυλάξεις ἃ παρέλαβες)." In non-Christian sources φυλάσσειν is found with παραθήκη (or παρακαταθήκη) in, e.g., Demosthenes *Against Meidias* 18.15; Philo *De inebr.* 52; Ps.-Socrates *Ep. 28.6* (Malherbe, *Cynic Epistles,* 288).

labor, you have me as your rest.[a] If you desire a friend who supplies goods not of this world, I am your friend. [6]If you desire a father for those who are rejected on earth, I am your father. If you desire a legitimate brother to set you apart from bastard brothers, I am your brother. [7]If you desire and seek anything more valuable to you, you have me with all that is mine and all that is mine will be in you.' Beloved, our Lord gives us this reply."

12:8 [a] → AAnMt3:3
[b]Cf. AAnMt 32:6

[8]After Andrew said these things, some of the brethren[a] cried, others rejoiced, but because he had become a neophyte,[b] Stratocles in particular was so excited in his mind that he gave up all his possessions and devoted himself to the word alone.

13:1 [a] → AAnMt 3:3
[b] → APaTh 5:1
[c] → 8:2

13 There was great joy[a] among the believers[b] as they got together night and day[c] at the praetorium with Maximilla. [2]On Sunday, when they were gathered in Aegeates's bedroom listening to Andrew, the proconsul arrived. [3]When her husband's arrival was announced to Maximilla she panicked, anticipating this outcome: that he would apprehend so many people inside.

[4]When Andrew saw her confusion, he said to the Lord, "Do not permit Aegeates to enter this bedroom, Lord Jesus, until your servants can leave here without fear; they've come together for your sake, and Maximilla constantly pleads with us to meet and get some rest here. [5]Because you have judged her worthy to deserve your kingdom, may she be especially emboldened, and Stratocles, too. [6]Save us all by repelling that savage lion armed to attack us."

13:8 [a] → AAnMt 3:3

[7]When the proconsul Aegeates came in, he got an urge for a bowel movement, asked for a chamber pot, and spent a long time sitting, attending to himself. [8]He did not notice all the believers[a] exiting right in front of him—Andrew had laid his hand on each one and had said, "Jesus will screen your appearance from Aegeates, so as to ensure your invisibility before him." [8]Last of all, Andrew sealed himself and left.

13:2 • *On Sunday* (κυριακῆς οὔσης), literally, "on the Lord's day"; see already Rev 1:10, and note on AcPetBG 1:1.
13:8 • *and left:* At this point the reader is to assume that only Aegeates is left in the bedroom. The next chapter, however, places him somewhere outside, presumably outside of the praetorium, and places Maximilla in her own bedroom "still asleep." This non sequitur may simply indicate the author's lack of narrative control, but it may also suggest that *HS* has failed to report an episode that interrupted these two chapters.

13:2 *arrived:* E adds "from the emperor"; GE "from Rome."

14 When this grace of the Lord was completed, Stratocles, because he had been away from his brother for a long time, went out and embraced Aegeates, with a smile on his face but with no joy in his soul. [2]The rest of his servants and freedmen greeted him in the same way. [3]But Aegeates, out of passion for Maximilla, rushed into the bedroom assuming she was still asleep—though instead she was praying. [4]And when she saw him, she looked away toward the ground.

[5]"First give me your right hand," he told her. "I will kiss the woman I will call no longer 'wife' but 'queen,' so that I may find relief in your chastity and love for me."

[6]This is what had happened: when the wretch caught her in her prayer, he supposed she was praying for him, being delighted to hear his own name mentioned while she prayed. [7]But this is what Maximilla actually said: "Rescue me at last from Aegeates's filthy intercourse and keep me pure and chaste, giving service only to you, my God." [8]So when he approached her mouth intending to kiss it, she pushed him back and said, "Aegeates, after prayer a woman's mouth should never touch a man's."

[9]Taken back by the sternness of her face, the proconsul left her. Because he had just completed a long journey, he put off his traveling clothes, relaxed, and lay down to sleep.

15 Maximilla then told Iphidama, "Sister, go to the blessed one so that he may come here to pray and lay his hand on me while Aegeates is sleeping."

[2]Without hesitation she ran to Andrew, and after she reported the request of faithful Maximilla, Andrew went and entered another bedroom where Maximilla was. [3]Stratocles also went in with the apostle, having come with the blessed one from his guest residence. [4](After Stratocles had greeted his brother, he had asked about the accommodations at which the Lord's apostle was staying; this is how, guided by a brother named Antiphanes, Stratocles got to enter with the blessed one.)

14:6 • *This is what had happened* translates the explanatory particle γάρ ("for"). The sentence explains why Aegeates makes the offer he has just made.
15:4 • The awkwardness of the preceding three sentences results from the absence in *HS* of any earlier reference to Antiphanes or anyone else entertaining Andrew in Patras. *M* 9 also mentions an Antiphanes as Andrew's host, and GE 29 mentions a wealthy man named Antiphanes apparently in Megara. These traces suggest that Antiphanes was more important in the ancient Acts than our sources allow us to see. Presumably, when Antiphanes and his wife converted in Megara (so GE), they became patrons to Andrew, traveled with him from Patras, and hosted him there (as in *HS M*).

16 Andrew laid his hand on Maximilla and prayed as follows: "I ask you, my God, Lord Jesus Christ, who knows the future, <and> I entrust to you my child, worthy Maximilla. ²May your word and power be mighty in her, and may the spirit that is in her prevail even against Aegeates, that insolent and hostile snake. ³Lord, may her soul remain forever pure, sanctified by your name—protect her especially, Master, from this disgusting pollution. ⁴As for him, our savage and perpetually boorish enemy: enable her to sleep apart from her visible husband and be wed to her inner husband. ⁵He it is that you above all recognize, and for whose sake the entire mystery of your plan of salvationᵃ has been accomplished. ⁶Since she has such a firm faith in you, may she attain her own proper kinship through separation from <those> masquerading <as friends> but <who are> actual enemies." ⁷When he had prayed like this and entrusted Maximilla to the Lord, he left with Stratocles once more.

16:5 ᵃ → AAnMt 2:5

17 Maximilla then planned the following. She summoned a shapely, notoriously wanton servant-girl named Euclia and told her what she delighted in and desired: ²"You will have me as a benefactor of all that you require, provided that you go along with my scheme and carry out what I tell you to do."

³Because she wanted to live chastely from that time on, Maximilla told Euclia what she wanted and got her word agreeing to it, and so for a while she employed this special subterfuge. ⁴Just as a woman customarily dresses herself up to look like her rival, so Maximilla groomed Euclia in her own finery and dispatched her to sleep with Aegeates in her stead. ⁵Having used her as his lover, he let her get up and go to her own bedroom, as Maximilla used to do. ⁶In this way Maximilla escaped detection for some time, and so got some relief, rejoiced in the Lord, and never left Andrew.

18 Eight months passed. But now Euclia demanded that her lady obtain her freedom for her; and that very day, Maximilla granted her what she asked. ²A few days later, she made more demands—this time a large sum of money—and again Maximilla gave in to her without hesitation; likewise, when Euclia demanded some of her

---

17:1–6 • Evodius of Uzala (*De fide contra Manichaeos* 38) paraphrases this chapter: "Maximilla . . . imposed on her husband her maidservant Euclia by making her up . . . with devious finery and cosmetics and by substituting her in her place at night, so that without knowing it he would sleep with her as with his wife."
17:1 • *and told her,* i.e., Maximilla told Euclia; or possibly Maximilla induces Euclia to tell her what she (Euclia) most desires.

jewelry, Maximilla did not object. ³But the simple truth of it is that, though Euclia regularly took clothing, fine linen, and headbands from Maximilla, she was not content with that, but flaunted the affair before the other servants, boasting like a show-off.

⁴The slaves, though irritated at Euclia's bragging, at first held back from lashing out at her. ⁵She, of course, would mock them when showing them the gifts her mistress had given her; at which Euclia's fellow servants would acknowledge them, but <knew they> were at a loss about what to do. ⁶So, wishing to provide even more proof of what she was saying, Euclia stationed two of them at the head of her master's bed when he was drunk, to convince them that she was indeed sleeping with him as though she were Maximilla. ⁷When she woke him from a deep sleep, she and the fellow servants looking on heard this: "Maximilla, my lady, why so late?" ⁸Euclia said nothing, and the attending servants left the bedroom without a peep.

19 Maximilla no doubt supposed that Euclia was true to her word, and to be trusted because of the gifts given her; and at night she took her rest with Andrew, along with Stratocles and all her fellow believers.ᵃ ²But it <just so> happened that Andrew had a vision, and he reported it to them (Maximilla was listening, too): ³"Today at the home of Aegeates some new plot is brewing, brimming with trouble and some sort of anger." ⁴Maximilla begged him to let on what this was about; but he <simply> said, "Don't be so eager to learn from me what you'll get to know soon enough!"

20 She changed <out of her> typical dress <into something different>, and now went in, with the praetorium gate in plain view. ²The household servants who had learned of the arrangement—how it was that every day she and Stratocles sneaked off to Andrew, and at what hour she returned to her own bedroom—took her for some out-of-towner. ³(She had sneaked into the proconsul's praetorium at that hour precisely to escape detection.) ⁴But when they had forcibly exposed her, they noticed she was their mistress. ⁵Some wanted to divulge the ruse and to tell everything to Aegeates; while others, ambivalent toward their mistress, feigned fondness for her and silenced the others—even assaulted them as though they were insane, and sent them away. ⁶While they were

19:1 ᵃ → AAnMt 3:3

20:6 • *burst into:* εἰσεπήδησεν (v.l. εἰσπηδᾶν); see also 51:3 (εἰσπηδῆσαι). The verb occurs in the NT only at Acts 16:29, when a Philippian jailer "rushes in" to meet Paul and Silas; in the LXX only at Amos 5:19; Sus 26.

fighting among themselves, Maximilla burst into her bedroom and prayed that the Lord would ward off every evil from her.

21 An hour later, those who had fought on Maximilla's behalf against their fellow-servants set upon her—fawning, looking for some payoff, as though they were servants of Aegeates. ²The blessed lady considered them deserving of their request and summoned Iphidama: "Let's give them their due," she said. ³So she ordered that those who had hypocritically simulated affection for her <each> be given one thousand denarii, and commanded them to disclose the matter to no one <else>.

21:4 ªCf. 40:2; 49:3;
Jn 8:44

⁴Even though they solemnly swore themselves to silence about what they had seen, at the instigation of their father the devilª they went to their master immediately, money in hand. ⁵They told him the whole story, including how their own fellow servant submitted to the plan Maximilla devised because she no longer wanted to sleep with Aegeates, repulsed by sex with him as a heinous and despicable act.

22 The proconsul learned everything in detail—how Euclia had shared his bed as though she were his spouse, and how she had confessed to having done so to her fellow slaves. ²Through interrogation he also discovered her motivation, because under torture she confessed to all the payoffs she had received from her lady for keeping quiet.

³The proconsul was furious at her for boasting to her fellow servants and for saying these things to defame her mistress. ⁴He wanted the matter hushed up, since he was still affectionate for his spouse, so he cut out Euclia's tongue, mutilated her, and ordered

22:5 ªCf. 54:8

her thrown outside. ⁵There she stayed, without food for several days, before she herself became food for the dogs.ª ⁶The rest of the servants who had told their story to him—there were three of them—he crucified.

23 Stricken by grief, Aegeates stayed in seclusion that day and ate nothing at all, baffled by the great change in Maximilla's attitude toward him. ²After crying for some time and reproaching his gods, he went to his spouse, fell at her feet in his tears: ³"I cling to your feet," he said, "I who have been your husband now for twelve

---

21:2 • *blessed lady:* μακαρῖτις, the feminine form of μακαρίτης, which commonly refers to the dead, or "dearly departed"; but in Christian writings it is also used absolutely as the feminine counterpart to μακάριος, "the blessed one."

years, who always revered you as a goddess and still do because of your chastity and your refined character, even though it may be tarnished somewhat since even you are human. [4]If you're keeping some secret from me about another man, something I would never have suspected, I'll make allowances—I'll cover it up myself, just as so often you have put up with my foolishness. [5]Or if there is something else, something even more serious, that separates you from me, confess it and I will quickly remedy the situation—I know <by now that> it's quite useless to contradict you."

[6]While he persistently cajoled and begged, she made her declaration to him: "I am in love, Aegeates; I am in love, but the object of my love is not of this world and therefore is imperceptible to you. [7]Night and day[a] it kindles and enflames me with love for it; but you can't see it, because it's difficult to see, and you cannot separate me from it, because that's impossible. [8]So then, let me have intercourse and take my rest with it alone."

23:7 [a] → 8:2

24 The proconsul left her like some maniac, not knowing what to do. He did not dare commit any impropriety against the blessed woman—her pedigree far outstripped his. [2]So he said to Stratocles, who was walking with him, "Brother, my only legitimate blood-relation now that our entire family has died off: I don't know if my wife is in a state of ecstasy or lunacy!"

[3]And as he dispiritedly began to tell Stratocles what he had to say, one of his attending servants whispered in his ear, "Master, if you would learn of this affair in detail, ask Stratocles; he will satisfy your curiosity, because he knows all about your wife. [4]But if you prefer to learn of the entire affair right now, I'll apprize you."

25 He drew Aegeates aside and told him privately, "There is a certain stranger sojourning here who has become renowned not only in this city but throughout Achaea. [2]He performs great miracles and cures with superhuman strength, as I in part can corroborate in that I was present and saw him revive corpses. [3]And—so that you may know the whole story—he proclaims a reverence for the divine and truly shows it to be shining forth in public view. [4]My mistress, following Iphidama's lead, got to know this stranger. [5]She has so given way to desire for him that she loves no one more than him—including you, I would say. [6]Not only has she become intimately involved with the man, she has tied up your brother

---

25:2 • *revive corpses:* A reference back to AcAndGE 24:15–29.

25:7 ᵃ → AAnMt 33:9

Stratocles with the same passion for him that has tied her up. ⁷They confess but one God,ᵃ the one that that man <Andrew> disclosed to them, and deny the existence of every other on earth. ⁸But listen to what your brother has done—the craziest thing of all: Even though he is of noble stock, the most honored man in Achaea, addressed as brother of the proconsul Aegeates, he carries his own little oil flask to the gymnasium. ⁹Even though he owns many slaves, he appears in public doing his own chores—buying his own vegetables, bread, and other supplies, and carrying them on foot through the center of the city—making himself look a simple object of shame to everyone."

26 As he was telling this to his master—Aegeates was taking a stroll, all the while staring at the ground—the young man spotted Andrew from a distance and shouted out loud: ²"Look, master! There's the man responsible for the present disruption of your household." The entire crowd turned to see the cause of his outburst. ³Without another word, the youth, who was as impassioned as Aegeates, as if his brother rather than his slave, ran from the proconsul, seized Andrew, and forcibly brought him to Aegeates, wrapping around his neck the towel that the blessed one used to wear over his shoulder.ᵃ

26:3 ᵃCf. ATh 106:4

⁴When the proconsul saw him, he recognized him: "You're the one who once cured my wife," he said, "and refused a considerable sum of money I wanted to donate. ⁵Teach me, too, what accounts for your renown—what sort of power you have, such that you have lovers, so I hear, who are rich and poor, including infants, even though you appear this way, like nothing but an old tramp."

⁶The entire crowd gathered there dearly loved the apostle, and when they learned that the proconsul was speaking with him, but not knowing why, they ran to where he was talking with Andrew. ⁷Without hesitation Aegeates ordered him locked up, saying, "Corrupter! You'll see my rewards to you for your benefactions to Maximilla."

26:3 • *as if his brother rather than his slave* (ὥσπερ καὶ αὐτοῦ ἀδελφός, οὐ γὰρ δὴ δοῦλος): Though the exact wording is rather different, an allusion to Phlm 16 is compelling: "no longer as a slave but more than a slave, as a beloved brother (οὐκέτι ὡς δοῦλον ἀλλ᾽ ὑπὲρ δοῦλον, ἀδελφὸν ἀγαπητόν)."

26:6–7 M 9b–10 gives a different account of the arrest of Andrew, in which the role of the crowd is much more significant. Instead of the slave-boy bringing Andrew to Aegeates, Aegeates sends his henchmen to arrest the apostle at the house of Antiphanes, Andrew's host.

27 A short time later, Aegeates left, went to Maximilla, and discovered her eating bread and olives with Iphidama—it was the right time for it—and said to her, [2]"Maximilla, now that I have captured your teacher and locked him up, I bring you news about him: he'll not escape from me but will suffer a horrible death."

[3]"My teacher isn't someone who can be held in check," the blessed lady answered, "because he can't be 'caught,' just as he can't be seen. [4]You've never had to overpower anyone like this, Aegeates, so stop this boasting."

[5]But he left anyway, smiling, and leaving her to eat.

[6]"Sister," Maximilla said to Iphidama, "here we are, eating, while our benefactor, second <only> to the Lord himself, is imprisoned. [6]Go to the garrison in the name of the Lord, Iphidama, and find out where the prison is. [7]I believe that at nightfall we will be able to see the Lord's apostle, and that no one will see me leaving except Jesus and you, my guide."

28 Iphidama changed out of her usual garb and dutifully rushed off. [2]Once she discovered where the prison was, she went there and saw a large crowd standing at the prison gate. [3]She asked around as to why the crowd had formed, and someone told her: "Because of the most pious Andrew, locked up by Aegeates."

[4]When faithful Iphidama had stood there for an hour, she saw the prison gate opened, and, encouraged by this, she said, "Jesus, I ask you to go in with me to your servant." [5]No one detected her as she went in and found the apostle speaking with his fellow inmates—he had already strengthened them, encouraging them to believe in the Lord.

29 When he turned and saw Iphidama, his soul was filled with joy: he said to the Lord, "Glory be to you, Jesus Christ, ruler of true words and promises, who instills courage in my fellow servants! [2]All who encounter you conquer their enemies, because you alone exist. [3]Look, your Iphidama, driven by desire for us, has come here; I know that she and her mistress are under surveillance. [4]Shield her with your covering both now as she leaves and this evening, when she returns with her mistress, so that they will be invisible to their enemies. [5]For as long as I have been here, they have made every effort to be bound together with me, so guard them yourself, Lord, for they are devoted lovers of God."

[6]Now, having prayed for Iphidama, Andrew let her go: "The prison gate will be opened before you get there," he said, "and

29:7 ªCf. Phil 4:4

when you and Maximilla return here this evening, it will have been opened again. [7]And you'll rejoice in the Lord[a] and leave again, so that by these events, too, you both may be confirmed in our Lord."

30 Iphidama left at once and found everything to be just as Andrew had predicted. [2]When she came to Maximilla, she reported to her the blessed one's noble soul and resolve; namely, that even though imprisoned he was not quiet but in fact urged on his fellow inmates and praised the Lord's power. [3]She also recounted to her everything else he had said to her inside the prison that both of them had reason to know about.

[4]When Maximilla had heard everything Iphidama could tell her about the apostle, she was overwhelmed by her joyful spirit: [2]"Glory be to you, O Lord," she said, "for I am about to see your apostle again without fear. [3]Even if an entire legion kept me under lock-and-key, it would not be strong enough to prevent me from seeing your apostle—it would be blinded by the radiant appearance of the Lord and by the boldness of his servant before God." [4]Having said this, she waited for lamps to be lit so that she could leave.

31 The proconsul said to some of those who were with him, "I do know of Maximilla's audacity—she never obeys me! [2]So do this: leave the praetorium doors unguarded, but have four men go off to the prison and tell the jailer, 'Right now, secure the door for which you are responsible! [3]See that you not open it for any of the dignitaries, even if you're won over by intimidation or bribery—not even if I should come myself—or you will be missing your head!'"

[4]He commanded four others posted around her bedroom to detect if she should come out. [5]The first four sped to the prison, while the others paced in front of the blessed woman's bedroom, as ordered; <and meanwhile> the accursed Aegeates went to supper.

32:1–4 Evodius of Uzala (*De fide contra Manichaeos* 38) seems to refer to this episode: "When this same Maximilla and Iphidama together went to hear the apostle Andrew, a beautiful child, whom Leucius wants to be taken as God or at least as an angel, brought them to the apostle Andrew, then went on to Aegeates's praetorium, entered their bedroom and mimicked a woman's voice to sound like Maximilla grumbling over the sufferings of the female sex, and Iphidama responding. When Aegeates heard this conversation, he thought they were there and went away."

HS seems to have omitted not only this story of Jesus' ventriloquism but a substantial speech as well. The last section of this speech is preserved in *Vaticanus gr. 808* (=*Vat*), a fragment of Andrew's passion that runs parallel to *HS* for the next several chapters.

32 Maximilla prayed with Iphidama to the Lord for a long time, telling the Lord again, "Lord, at last it's time for me to go to your servant." [2]She left the bedroom with Iphidama, saying, "Lord, be with us and <please> don't forsake those who are here."

[3]When she arrived at the prison gate, she found a beautiful young boy standing before opened doors, who told them, "Both of you go in to your Lord's apostle who has been expecting you for some time." [4]Running ahead of them, he went to Andrew and told him, "Look, Andrew, these women have come to you rejoicing in your Lord. May they be strengthened in him by your speech."

Vaticanus gr. 808 (= Vat; chapter numbers in parentheses) continues with the end of the speech:

33 (1) " . . .] is everything about you lax? Have you still not convinced yourselves that you don't yet bear his goodness? [2]Let us stand in awe and rejoice with one another over our abundant partnership with him. Let us say <this> to one another:

[3]"Blessed is our race, for someone has loved it.
    Blessed is our existence, for someone has shown it mercy.
[4]We are not cast to the ground,
    for we have been recognized by such a height.
[5]We do not belong to time,
    so as to be dissolved by time.
[6]We are not the product of motion, which disappears of its own accord,
    nor <of> the cause of coming-to-be,
    so as to wind up in the same condition.
[7]Rather, we are those who aspire to greatness:
    We belong to the one who actually shows mercy.
[8]We belong to the better: therefore we flee the worse.
    We belong to the good, through <whom> we shove aside the disgraceful;
[9]to the just, through whom we reject the unjust;
    to the merciful, through whom we abandon the unmerciful;
[10]to the Savior, through whom we have recognized the destroyer;
    to the light, through whom we have cast off the darkness;
[11]to the one, through whom we have turned from the many;
    to the heavenly, through whom we have learned about the earthly;

¹²to the enduring,

through whom we see things that do not endure.'

¹³[There is no more] worthy [reason for our] resolving to give thanks, to speak boldly, to sing a hymn, or to boast before the God who had mercy on us than that we have been recognized by him."

34 (2) And after he had spoken with the women for some time, at last he sent them away, saying, "Go in peace. ²You know very well, maidservants of Christ, that because of his love I will never fully leave you, and that because of his mediation, you will never again abandon me." Each one left for home.

34:3 ᵃ → APaTh 5:1

³For several days, while Aegeates had no thought of pressing charges against the apostle, there was great joyᵃ among them. ⁴Every day they were strengthened in the hope of the Lord, and they got together fearlessly at the prison. ⁵They were almost always with Maximilla and Iphidama and the others, because they were screened by the covering and grace of the Lord.

35 (3) But one day, while Aegeates sat as judge, he remembered his business with Andrew. ²Like a maniac, he left the case at hand, rose from the bench, and dashed to the praetorium, seething with fury at Maximilla—but flattering her all the same! ³(Maximilla had come home from the prison before he arrived.)

36 (4) When he got near her, he said, "Maximilla, because your parents thought me worthy to be your mate, they pledged you to me in marriage without regard to wealth, heredity, or reputation, considering only the kindness of my soul. ²Just now I intentionally left the court and came here, not to enumerate the many matters I had wanted to bring forth to your disgrace—benefits I enjoyed from your parents, honors and favors you received from me during our entire lives, your designation as my queen—but simply to learn

36:3 ᵃCf. 64:7

from you this one thing. ³If you would be the woman you once were, living together with me as was so familiar to us—sleeping with me, having sex with me, conceiving children with meᵃ—I would treat you well in every way. ⁴What's more, I'll release the stranger I have in prison. ⁵But if you should not choose this course, I will do you no

---

33:12 *do not endure:* "not" is supplied to continue the contrast between "heavenly" and "earthly" in the previous line.

33:13 Words in brackets are supplied to fill a short lacuna in the ms.

harm—I am unable to—but I'll torment you indirectly through the one you love more than me. [6]Answer me tomorrow, Maximilla, after you have considered which of the two options you want: I'm fully prepared to carry out this threat."

[7]And having said this, he left.

37 (5) At the usual time, Maximilla again went with Iphidama to Andrew. [2]Putting his hands on her eyes and then bringing them to her mouth, she kissed them and began to seek his advice about every aspect of Aegeates's ultimatum.

[3]"Maximilla, my child," Andrew replied, "I know that you too have been moved to resist any proposition of sexual intercourse and wish to be disassociated from so foul and filthy a way of life. [4]For a long time this conviction has dominated my thinking, but still you want me to bear witness to my intent. [5]I bear you witness, Maximilla: do not commit this act. Don't submit to Aegeates's threat. Don't be moved by his speech. [6]Don't fear his disgusting schemes. Don't be conquered by his artful flatteries. Don't consent to yield yourself to his filthy wizardry. [7]Endure each of his tortures by looking at us for a while, and you will see him entirely numb and wasting away from you and from all of your relatives. [8]And, since I'm not keeping silent about making the matter visible and actual through you, the most important thing I must tell you now comes to me: [9]I rightly see in you Eve repenting and in me Adam converting. For what she suffered through ignorance, you—whose soul I seek—must now redress through conversion. [10]The very thing suffered by the mind which was brought down with her and slipped away from itself, I make right with you, through your recognition that you are being raised up. [11]You have healed her deficiency by not experiencing the same passions, and I have perfected Adam's imperfection by fleeing to God for refuge. [12]What Eve disobeyed, you obeyed; what Adam agreed to, I flee; the things that tripped them up, we have recognized. It is ordained that each person correct his or her own fall.[a]

38 (6) "Having said these things as I said them, I would also say this:

[2]Well done, nature being saved,
   because you are neither overbearing nor in hiding.
[3]Well done, soul crying out what you suffered
   and returning to yourself.

37:12 [a]Cf. ATh 15:6; 30:1

⁴Well done, human who learns what is not yours
    and speeds on to what is yours.
⁵Well done, hearer of what is being said:
    I know that you are greater than what is thought or said.

⁶I recognize that you are more powerful than those who presume to dominate you; more distinguished than those who cast you down to shame, than those who lead you away to captivity. ⁷O human being, if you understand all these things in yourself—that you are immaterial, holy, light, akin to the unbegotten, intellectual, heavenly, transparent, pure, beyond the flesh, beyond the world, beyond the powers, beyond the authorities over whom you really are— ⁸if you comprehend yourself in your condition, if you perceive with the mind through which you excel, if you see your face in your essence, having broken every shackle— ⁹I mean not only those shackles acquired by coming-into-being but also those beyond the realm of coming-into-being, whose magnificent names we have presented to you— ¹⁰then desire to see him who was revealed to you without coming into being, whom you alone will soon recognize, if you take courage.

39 (7) "I have said these things in your presence, Maximilla, because the force of what has been said extends also to you. ²Just as Adam died in Eve through his complicity with her, so too I now live in you through your observing the commandment of the Lord and through your transporting yourself to a state worthy of your essence. ³Scorn Aegeates's threats, Maximilla, for you know that we have a God who has compassion on us. Do not let his blatherings move you, but remain chaste. ⁴Let him not only avenge himself on me with the tortures of captivity, let him also throw me to the beasts, burn me with fire, and throw me off a cliff. So what? ⁵Let him destroy this body if that's what he wants—it is only one body, and it is akin to him.

40 (8) "Once again I have a speech for you, Maximilla: I say to you, do not yield yourself to Aegeates. ²Stand up against his traps, especially, Maximilla, since I saw the Lord saying to me, 'Andrew, Aegeates's father the devil[a] will use him to release you from this prison.' ³So from now on keep yourself chaste and pure, holy, unsullied, unalloyed, unadulterated, unassociated with anything foreign

40:2 ᵃCf. 21:4; 49:3; Jn 8:44

40:3 ᵃCf. Gn 4:1–16; 1 Jn 3:12

39:2 • *your essence*, or "being" (οὐσία).

to us, unbroken, undamaged, unweeping, unwounded, untroubled by storms, undivided, unfalling, unsympathetic to the works of Cain.ᵃ ⁴For if you do not give yourself up to their opposites, Maximilla, I will rest, even if I am forcibly let go from this life for your sake—that is, for my sake. ⁵If I am driven from here, perhaps I can help others of my kindred because of you, but if you become won over by the seductions of Aegeates and the flatteries of the serpent, his father, so that you return to your former sexual acts, know this: ⁶I will be punished there because of you, until you yourself realize that I despised living this life because of an unworthy soul.

41 (9) "Therefore, I beg you, wise man, that your clear-sighted mind stand firm. I beg you, mind unseen, that you may be protected. I entreat you, love Jesus. ²Do not be overcome by the inferior. You whom I entreat as a man, assist me in my becoming perfect. ³Help me too, so that you may recognize your true nature. Suffer with my suffering, so that you may recognize what I suffer and escape suffering. ⁴See what I see, and what you see will blind you. See what you should, and you will not see what you should not. ⁵Hear what I say and throw off whatever you heard <from Aegeates>. I have said these things to you and to anyone who's listening, if you'll hear <them>.

42 (10) "But to you, Stratocles," he said, looking at him, "why are you afflicted with many tears and why do you groan out loud? Why do you despair? Why your great grief and great sorrow? ²You recognize what has been said, so why do I beg you, child, that you live accordingly? Do you know to whom I've said these things? ³Has each engaged your mind? Has it reached your intellectual faculty? Do I still have the one who listened to me? ⁴Do I find myself in you? Is there someone in you speaking whom I see as my own? ⁵Does he love the one who has spoken in me, and does he desire to have fellowship with him? Does he wish to be united with him? Does he strive to become loved by him? ⁶Does he long to be yoked with him? Does he find any rest in him? Does he have anywhere to lay his

42:6 ᵃCf. AAnMt 16:1; Mt 8:20; Lk 9:58

41:1 • *wise man:* τοῦ φρονίμου ἀνδρός, a striking expression since the noun ἀνήρ usually stands for a grown male, in contrast to women or boys. Possibly the phrase is inspired by Matt 7:24, the only place in the NT where φρόνιμος and ἀνήρ occur in combination, in which the "wise man" builds his house on rock: likewise Maximilla as "the wise man" is to have her mind "stand firm." Alternatively, Maximilla has in a sense become male to repel her husband's advances.
41:2 • *as a man:* Here the word is ἄνθρωπος ("person"), which often stands in contrast to gods or animals.

head?[a] [7]Surely there's nothing in you to resist him—nothing to be resistant to him, nothing to counteract him, nothing to hate him, nothing to escape from him, nothing to be savage to him, nothing to shun him, nothing that has turned away from him, nothing to rush from him, nothing to be oppressed, nothing to fight him, nothing to associate with others, nothing to be flattered by others, nothing to conspire with others, [8]no other things to disturb him, nothing in you alien to me, no opponent, no corrupter, no enemy, no magician, no charlatan, no pervert, no deceiver, no traitor, no misanthrope, no hater of rational discourse, no one like a tyrant, no boaster, no snob, no maniac, no kindred of the snake, no weapon of the devil, no advocate for fire, no property of darkness—is there? [9]Stratocles, surely there's no one in you to oppose my saying these things, is there? Who is it? Answer! [10]I don't speak in vain, do I? I haven't spoken in vain, have I? 'No!' says the person in you who weeps once again, Stratocles."

43 (11) Then Stratocles came forward to Andrew, weeping and wailing. [2]So Andrew took Stratocles's hand and said, "I have the one I sought. I have found the one I desired. I hold the one I loved. I rest because of the one I have waited for. [3]The very fact that you are groaning still louder and crying uncontrollably symbolizes for me that I have already achieved rest, because it cannot have been in vain that I spoke to you the words that are akin to me."

44 (12) "Most blessed Andrew," Stratocles replied, "don't think that there is anything that bothers me but you, for the words that came from you are like flaming javelins impaling me: each of them strikes me and actually blazes and burns with love for you. [2]The sensitive part of my soul, the part that inclines towards the things I've heard, is tormented—it can predict the grief that comes with them. [3]For you yourself will go away, and I know well enough that it's good that you do. But after that, where and in whom will I seek and find your concern and love? [4]I received the seeds of the words of salvation[a] while you were my sower; for them to shoot up and reproduce requires no one else but you, blessed Andrew.[b] What can I say to you but this, servant of God? [5]I need the great compassion and help that come from you so as to be worthy of these seeds I already have from you; otherwise, I might not see them undamaged,

44:4 [a]Cf. Ac 13:26; ATh 94:1
[b]Cf. Mk 4:1–20; Mt 13:1–23; Lk 8:1–15

sprouting into the open, if you weren't willing it and praying for them and for the whole of me."

45 (13) "Child," answered Andrew, "these things are what I myself also found in you. I glorify my Lord that my estimation of you was not groundless, but knew what it was talking about. ²This is how you'll know it: tomorrow Aegeates will hand me over to be impaled on a stake. ³Maximilla, the Lord's servant, will trouble the enemy in him to whom he belongs, and will not consent with him to do anything alien to her. By turning against me he will presume to console himself."

46 (14) Maximilla was not present when the apostle said this, for when she had heard the <earlier> words that applied to her she was somehow changed by them: she became what the words themselves had signified. ²She rushed out deliberately and resolutely and went to the praetorium. ³Because she had said goodbye to her whole life as well as to wickedness, the mother of the flesh, and to things belonging to the flesh,ᵃ when Aegeates brought up his usual reprehensible ultimatum, which he had told her to ponder—namely, whether she would be willing to sleep with him—she rebuffed him. ⁴And so he turned attention at last to the destruction of Andrew, and began to consider what kind of death he might impose on him;ᵃ of all the options, crucifixion most attracted him. ⁵Then he went off with his cronies and ate like a wild animal.

47 (15) Maximilla—the Lord now going ahead of her, looking exactly like Andrew—went to the prison again with Iphidama. ²A great crowd of believersᵃ was inside, when she found him saying this: "Brothers and sisters, the Lord sent me as an apostle to these regions of which my Lord considered me worthy— ³not to teach anyone, but to remind everyone akin to these words that all people pass their time among ephemeral evils, reveling in their destructive fantasies, things I have continually encouraged you to shun.

46:3 ᵃCf. Rom 8:5

46:4 ᵃCf. 51:2

47:2 ᵃ → AAnMt 3:3

45:2 • *impaled on a stake* is probably the equivalent of crucifixion; see 46:4.
46:1 • *words that applied to her*, i.e., Andrew's address to Maximilla in 37:3–41:5.
46:4 • *crucifixion:* ἀνασκολοπισθῆναι, more literally, "impaling on a stake"; see 45:2.
47:1 • *the Lord . . . Andrew* (προηγουμένου αὐτῆς τοῦ κυρίου ἰδέᾳ τοῦ Ἀνδρέα), or possibly "led by the Lord disguised as Andrew"; cf. AcPaulThec 21; AcThom 11:3.

⁴I've urged you to pursue whatever is stable, and to get away from everything that won't stay still. ⁵But look at you! Not one of you can stand firm: everything, including human conventions, is in flux. ⁶This happens because of the uneducated soul's wandering into nature and retaining <only> the <empty> pledges of its mistake. ⁷So I consider fortunate those who have obeyed the preached words, and who observe through them, as if in a mirror, the mysteries of their proper nature, for the sake of which everything was constructed.

48 (16) "Therefore I command you, beloved children: build firmly on the foundation laid for you—it's unshakable, and invulnerable to the stratagems of everyone who wishes you ill. ²Be planted on this foundation. Stand firm, remembering everything that happened while I was living with all of you.ᵃ ³You have seen deeds performed through me which you yourselves cannot disbelieve—signs done that even mute nature will surely have cried out to applaud. ⁴I have handed over to you words that I pray you received in the way the words themselves would require. ⁵Dear friends, stand firm in everything you have seen, heard, and shared in, and God, in whom you have believed because he had mercy, will present you to himself as acceptable, forever at rest.

49 (17) "Don't let what will to happen to me trouble you as if it were some strange surpriseᵃ—that God's servant, the one God has used to bring about many things through acts and words, will be driven from this passing life violently, and by a wicked man. ²This violence won't come on me alone, but on everyone who has loved and believed and confessed <Jesus>. ³The devil—ruthless, shameless as ever—will arm his own childrenᵃ against them, to join forces with him. But he'll not get what he wants. So why does he even try? I'll tell you: ⁴From the beginning of all things, or rather, from the time when the one without beginning descended to the realm

48:2 ᵃ → 41:1

49:1 ᵃCf. Jn 14:27; 1 Pt 4:12

49:3 ᵃCf. 21:4; 40:2; Jn 8:44

49:4 • *the one without beginning* (ὁ ἄναρχος): An attribute of Jesus Christ elsewhere attested in the early period, e.g., Clement of Alexandria *Strom.* 7.1 "the timeless and unoriginated (ἄναρχον) First Principle (ἀρχήν), and Beginning [or: first-fruits; ἀπαρχήν] of things that exist—the Son."
the realm beneath him: Probably a reference to the earth (as the realm beneath heaven); but possibly the underworld, as the realm visited by Christ between his death and resurrection (cf. 1 Pet 3:19).

49:4 *Vat* is defective; Arm "came to earth that he might drive <the devil> from us and destroy him."

beneath him to drive away [. . .]. ⁵The enemy, a stranger to peace, doesn't <oppress> what belongs to him, but one of the weaker, inconspicuous, and so far unidentifiable <believers>; and because this person doesn't understand <what is happening>, it seems to him necessary to wage war with <the enemy>. ⁶The explanation is that the enemy aspires to dominate him forever: he opposes him in a way that makes their hostility resemble a friendship. ⁷To get him under his control, he often flaunts his own pleasure-loving and deceitful traits, supposing that through these he will subjugate him. ⁸By faking a friendship befitting his victim, he doesn't display himself openly as an enemy.

50 (18) "This activity takes place for so long that the victim forgets to look out for it. ²<The devil>, of course, knows what's going on—that is, because of his gifts he <is not seen to be an enemy>. ³But when the mystery of grace was set aflame, and the plan for rest was revealed, and the light of the word was set forth, and the race being saved was proved to have been previously at war with pleasures; ⁴and when the enemy saw himself scorned and his gifts, through which he thought he could entrap <people>, ridiculed because of the goodness of the merciful one—then he began to entangle us in hate, hostility, and insurrection. ⁵He has made it his business not to leave us alone until we give way to the things that he values. ⁶For all the while this was the case, our opponent had nothing to worry about, and he pretended to depict his status as friendly to us: he had no fear that we would revolt, because we had been deceived by him. ⁷But let us not stand back from Christ through the deceit of

---

49:5 • *doesn't <oppress>:* I.e., for this author, the devil does not seek to defeat his own, but Christians of weak character.

49:5 • The sense appears to be that "the enemy" (i.e., the devil) is approached by the believer as an adversary; but in 49:6 the believer is disarmed, since the enemy appears to be a friend. This interpretation is not certain, however, since Arm takes the one who "wages war" to be "the Lord" (i.e., Jesus).

49:6 • *the explanation is:* γάρ, giving the reason for what has been stated before.

49:7 • *flaunts:* Here and in the following verse the main verbs are in the aorist tense, but expressing "the enemy's" standard mode of operation; hence the translation in the present tense.

49:5 Arm "And since the Lord came to wage war against him who was thought to be submerged in the abyss of hell, having fallen from glory and power, our creator God acquainted us with his father of eternal glory, that we might love him and do his commandments. I have written you many times about the base deceit of the troublemaker."

50:7 These last two sentences appear only in Arm. *Vat* is corrupt at this point: "But when the matter of God's plan (οἰκονομία) was kindled, I do not say stronger [. . .]" (cf. v. 3).

the enemy, because <now> the providence of God has been revealed to us and has enlightened us. He has weakened the enemy's power and arrogance. [8]For the hidden aspect of <the devil's> nature, and what seemed to be unnoticed—this Christ has exposed and forced to confess what it was. [9]Therefore, my brothers and sisters,[a] since we understand what will happen, let us wake up and separate ourselves from him. [10]Let us not be annoyed or agitated by the storm, and let us not carry along on our souls traces of <the devil> which are not ours. [11]We have been entirely buoyed up by the whole word, so let us all eagerly anticipate the goal, and let us get away from him, so that at last he may be exposed for what he is by nature, as we fly off to those things which are properly ours."

50:9 [a] → AAnMt 3:3

Here what is traditionally regarded as the *Martyrdom* begins (chapter numbers in parentheses):

51:1 [a] → AAnMt 3:3

51:2 [a]Cf. 46:4
[b]Cf. 1 Pt 2:11

51:3 [a]Cf. 20:6

51:5 [a]Cf. 54:7

51:6 [a]Cf. AAnMt 20:8
[b]Cf. 56:1

51 (1) All night long Andrew addressed the believers[a] like this and prayed, and everyone rejoiced together and was confirmed in the Lord. [2]Early next morning Aegeates summoned Andrew from prison and told him, "The time to complete my judgment against you has arrived,[a] you stranger, alien to this present life,[b] enemy of my home and corrupter of my entire house. [3]Why did you decide to burst into[a] places alien to you and corrupt a wife who used to please me in every way and never slept with another man? [4]She has convinced me that she now rejoices in you and your God. So enjoy my gifts!"

[5]He commanded that Andrew be flogged with seven whips. Then he sent him off to be crucified and commanded the executioners not to impale him with nails but to stretch him out tied up with ropes, <and> to leave his knees uncut,[a] supposing that by so doing he would punish Andrew even more cruelly.

[6]This became known to everyone, because the news spread throughout Patras that the stranger, the righteous one,[a] the man who possessed God, was being crucified by the impious Aegeates, even though he had done nothing improper. All alike were outraged.[b]

52 (2) As the executioners led him to the place, intending to carry out their orders, Stratocles, who had learned what was happening, arrived running and saw the executioners violently dragging off the blessed one like a criminal. [2]He did not spare any of them but gave each a beating, ripping their clothing from top to bottom, and tore Andrew away, telling them, "Thank the blessed one for educating me and teaching me to check my violent temper. [3]Otherwise, I would have shown you just what Stratocles—and <not only> Aegeates the rogue!—are capable of. For we <believers> have learned to endure our afflictions." [4]He grabbed the apostle's hand and went away with him to the seaside place where he was to be hung up.

53 (3) The soldiers left and presented themselves to Aegeates to explain what had happened. [2]"Change your clothes," the proconsul answered, "and go back there to perform your duties. Rid yourselves of the convict's friends, then obey your orders. [3]Avoid as best you can letting Stratocles see you, and don't argue about anything he requires of you—I know the nobility of his soul, such that if provoked he probably wouldn't even spare me." They did exactly as Aegeates told them.

[4]Stratocles walked with the apostle to the designated spot, but he was agitated, furious with Aegeates, now and then railing against him under his breath.

[5]"Stratocles, my child," Andrew responded, "from now on I want you to keep your mind firm, and don't wait for advice from someone else, but take such advice from yourself: [6]not to be inwardly oriented toward seeming hardships nor attached to mere appearances, for it is fitting for a servant of Jesus to be worthy of Jesus. [7]And I'll tell you and the believers[a] walking with me something else about people alien to us. [8]So long as the demonic nature lacks its bloody food and cannot suck up its nutrition when animals are not slain, it weakens and recedes to nothingness, becoming entirely dead. [9]But if it gets what it longs for, it firms up, expands, and rises up, growing by means of those foods it enjoys. [10]This, child, is what it's like for those outside who die when we <believers> are not attached to what they're attached to. [11]But even that self within ourselves which is contrary <to our true nature>, when it dares to do

53:7 [a] → AAnMt 3:3

53:3 *nobility* (εὐγενές): Ma and two mss of Arm read προπετές ("rashness").

something and cannot find anyone to consent with it, is beaten and totally crushed to the ground, dead, because it did not complete what it undertook. [12]Let us keep this image always before our eyes, children, so that we don't get drowsy and let the opponent come in and slaughter us."

At this point the Armenian Passion continues with an extended simile of an eagle. N and E also may reflect this passage: "Let us strive to renew the inner human, to let it fly to God in whom is all our desire." The best evidence for the inclusion of this speech comes from a similar speech comparing the soul with an eagle in Act 3 of the *Acts of Philip*, which almost certainly relies on a text of the *Acts of Andrew* that contained this discourse. It would therefore appear that Arm is our most reliable witness to this passage, though it would be unwise to look to it for precise fidelity.

[13]"I will tell you other things, because you have arrived at the end of the road before you, and because the demons have pitched battle against us on account of the sweet and pleasant commandments of God. [14]It seems to me that <the situation we are in> is like the regal bird, the eagle, that flies from earth on high, and is adorned with the rays of sunlight, by nature high-flying, appearing adorned with radiant beauty. [15]If <this bird>, soaring with light wings, flies around the earth, having left the usual traveling orbit of those living in light, it is corrupted by the earth, and its wings grow heavy. [16]And the eagle is actually transfigured, for although its nature is suited to the earth, nesting is unbecoming to its wings; when drawn to earth, it appears ridiculous to those who see it.

53:17 [a] → AAnMt 3:3   [17]"Such things, brothers and sisters,[a] are also known to us about our nature. When, like the eagle, we fly toward our natural heavenly light and adorn ourselves with the luminous commandments and the virtues of the spiritual, we shall be levitated by these and made to glow from natural lanterns and to be radiant with the growth of the plant of our beautiful and spiritual wings. [18]Like the eagle, as the soul makes its ascent to heaven on high it becomes visible to everyone, proud of its own wings, a pleasure for the eyes to look at, appearing beautiful up above to people below. [19]So too, we shall ascend to the heights and not be weighed down by any of our opponents, by dint of our virtue having shown good conduct, each in his or her appropriate course. [20]With humble thoughts we shall appear chosen, practicing various virtues, and these words will be written: that each one will know what is good for him or her, since the thoughts of the evil one are atrocious and disrespectful, and he hastens to make us lax in our will to do what God requires. [21]For we mortals were admonished by heavenly laws to avoid evil deeds, and to renew in our natures our good work; perhaps, then, we might 'take wing' like the example of the eagle of nature, which was renewed again.

[22]"I will explain to you this parable: When it appears that someone is well-endowed and radiant, then he will rise from the dead. Then a person appears worthy to all who see him, with splendid beauty going up to the Lord. [23]But if he remains on earth, he will appear the most humble—a joke to common fowl—for he will make himself resemble the lowliest bird.

[24]"And now I will tell you this about my 'eagle.' I established as an ideal for myself this much virtue, following the example of the perfectly just. [25]For they are crowned before all the world, and will put off the earthly body and the next time arise clothed in heavenly glory; and then into coveted paradise they will enter, rejoicing with the angels in the infinite joy of God.

[26]"This is the end of my speech—I think that while we were speaking we arrived at the designated place. [27]That's my sign: the cross planted there, pointing out the spot."

54 (4) He left everyone, approached the cross, and spoke to it out loud: "Greetings, O cross! Yes, greetings! [2]I know well that, though you have been weary for a long time, fixed here and waiting for me, you too can now rest at last. [3]I come to you, whom I have known: I recognize your mystery, why you were fixed there. [4]So then, cross that is pure, radiant, full of life and light, receive me, I who have been weary for so long."

53:21 • *eagle of nature*, i.e., the phoenix.

54:1–4 This address to the cross conforms with what one can reconstruct with confidence from HS AA Ma E Cd Ep. Other witnesses, however, greatly expand the speech, especially M and L (derived from a common source), Arm, and N (which for the most part goes its own way). Similarities between Arm and the Greek recensions M and L

surely derive from an even earlier stage of textual transmission, possibly from the ancient *Acts of Andrew* itself. A reconstruction of the extended speech appears on pp. 113–15.

54:3 *whom I have known:* M Arm L add "as my own"; one ms of M (echoed in N Cd Ep) and Arm also add "I come to you who long for me."

54:6 ª → AAnMt 3:3

54:7 ªCf. 51:5

54:8 ªCf. 22:5

55:1 ª → AAnMt 3:3

56:1 ªCf. 51:6

⁵The most blessed one said these things standing on the ground, looking intently at the cross. ⁶When he came to it, he commanded the believersª to summon the executioners, who were standing at some distance away, to carry out their orders. ⁷When they came, they tied up only his feet and armpits, without nailing up his hands or feet or severing his knees, because of what the proconsul had commanded them.ª ⁸(Aegeates, of course, intended to torment him by having him hanged this way, and eaten by dogsª if still alive at night.)

55 (5) The believersª were standing around, so many that they were nearly innumerable, and saw that the executioners had pulled back and had carried out against the blessed one none of the usual procedures suffered by those who are to be hanged. ²So they expected to hear something more from him, because even while hanging there he shook his head and smiled.

³"Why do you smile, Andrew, servant of God?" asked Stratocles. "Shouldn't your laughter make us mourn and weep because we are being deprived of you?"

⁴"Can't I laugh, Stratocles, my child," Andrew answered, "at Aegeates's futile trap by which he presumes to avenge himself on us? He hasn't yet been persuaded that we are alien to him and his designs. ⁵He isn't able to hear; if he were, he would have heard that, in the end, the person who belongs to Jesus and who has been recognized by him cannot be punished."

56 (6) When Andrew had said these things, he addressed a general speech to everyone, because even the pagans had hurried to the site, infuriated at Aegeates's unjust decision:ª ²"Men who are here with me, women, children, old, slaves, free, and any others who will listen: if you suppose this act of dying is <only> the end of ephemeral life, leave this place at once. ³If you understand the

---

55:2 • *smiled* (μειδιῶν): Smiling often denotes special insight or foreknowledge; see note on AcAndGE 16:3. In addition, in the *Phaedo* Plato repeatedly uses the same verb for the smiling Socrates the day of his death.
55:4 • *Can't I laugh . . .?* (οὐ μὴ γελάσω . . .): See notes on AcPaulThec 4:1; AcPetBG 1:7.
56:1 • *general speech*, i.e., a public discourse (κοινὸν λόγον), in contrast to the earlier private instruction; or possibly "extemporary" (LSJ, *s.v.* κοινός III.4 [p. 969a]), as the situation presumably would have required.
the pagans (τὰ ἔθνη), i.e., non-Christians.

56:2 Arm (perhaps correctly) "Behold I renounce this life"; *Ep* 2 "abandon this entire life."

conjunction of the soul with a body to be the soul itself, so that after the separation <of the two> nothing at all exists, you possess the intelligence of animals and you must be counted along with ferocious beasts. ⁴If you love immediate pleasures and pursue them above all, so as to enjoy their fruits exclusively, you are just like thieves. ⁵If you suppose that you're merely what can be seen and nothing more, you are slaves of folly and ignorance. ⁶If you reckon that only this nocturnal light exists and nothing in addition to it, you are kindred to this night. ⁷If you think that your earthly food <on its own> is capable of creating bodily mass and the blood's constitutive power, you yourselves are earthly. ⁸If you suppose that you're happy even though you have a body that's out of balance, actually you're miserable. ⁹If your external prosperity makes you happy, then for sure you are most wretched. ¹⁰If the pleasure and intercourse of marriage please you, even though the corruption that comes from them, full of pain, makes you sad; and if you're in need of sustenance for your many children, and if you're familiar with the bothersome poverty they cause, these desires will upset you. ¹¹And if the rest of your possessions draw you to themselves as though you belonged to them, may their impermanence reproach you!

57 (6 cont.) "After all, what benefit is there for you who gain for yourselves external goods but don't gain your very selves?ᵃ ²What pride is there in external ancestry if the soul within you is held captive, sold to desires?ᵃ ³And why do we wish the pleasure and childbearing <that marriage entails>, when later we have to separate? No one knows what he or she is doing. ⁴Who will take care of his wife when he's preoccupied only with the passions of desire? Or why all the other concern for externals, while you neglect what you yourselves actually are? ⁵Learn <from me>! I exhort you all instead to rid yourselves of this life which is painful, vain, crazy, boastful, empty, perishable, transitory, the friend of pleasures, the slave of time, the servant of drunkenness, the sojourner in debauchery, the possession of greed, the kindred of wrath, the umpire of treachery, the ally of murders, the prince of hatred, the patron of desire, the master of adulteries, the mediator of jealousies, the instigator of murders. ⁶I beg you, you who have come here together for my sake:

57:1 ᵃCf. Mk 8:36; Mt 16:26; Lk 9:25
57:2 ᵃCf. Rm 7:14

56:6 • *kindred to this night* (συγγενεῖς τῆς νυκτὸς ταύτης): Cf. AcThom 34:10 τὸν τῆς νυκτὸς συγγενῆ.
57:2 • *external ancestry*, i.e., physical lineage.

57:9 ᵃ → ATh 28:2

57:11 ᵃCf. 61:2

⁷Give up this entire life and hurry to overtake my soul which speeds toward things beyond time—⁸beyond law, speech, body, the bitter and lawless pleasures that are painful in every way. ⁹You, now, picture with the eyes of your soulsᵃ what I'm talking about. ¹⁰Follow in my deep-seated love; learn of my sufferings, which I'm telling you about now; take my mind as a down payment; make your fellowship with another community. ¹¹Wrap yourselves with my lashes, and clear your ears to hear what I say. Get away from everything that's merely temporal:ᵃ right now, come quickly away with me!

58 (6 *cont.*) "I can tell that you're being attentive to my words! I really can see you becoming gentle, the way I wish you to be, and far removed from external forms, because our unity is in what is internal. ²I greet you with the grace of God and with love that is due him and even more with your consent to each other. ³Keep yourselves from those who do harm, and attach yourselves to him, and to what is good: to the innocence that is in him, and to the accord that is in <what is good>. ⁴For this reason, men, quietly take courage in the knowledge of our God. ⁵For those who align themselves with me and are equipped with a pure faith and love for him, I am leaving to prepare their routes <to God>:ᵃ ⁶I am stifling the fire, banishing the shadows, extinguishing the furnace, killing the worm, eradicating the threat, gagging the demons, muzzling and destroying the ruling powers, dominating the authorities, throwing down the devil, casting out Satan, and punishing wickedness. ⁷But there are others, who came here not out of love for God but out of hypocrisy and because of unfruitful pleasures: ⁷those who have submitted themselves to superstition, disbelief, and every other ignorance, and who suppose nothing else exists after their release from here—that all these monsters fly out, become agitated, rush away, take wing, ravage, fight, conquer, rule, wreak vengeance, enflame, rage, afflict, punish, and attack. ⁸They blaze, act violently, and don't pull back or relent but rejoice, exult, smile, mock, and <then> take their rest and delight in all who are similar to them, possessing those who succumbed to them by not believing in my

58:5 ᵃCf. Jn 14:2, 6

58:4 • *men:* ἄνδρες (ἀνήρ) usually suggests a group of males only, e.g., in Mark 6:44 (hence the addition of "women and children" in Matt 14:21); see 58:9, and note on 41:1. Possibly the usage here reflects less the gender of the audience, which presumably comprises a mixed group of "pagans" (56:1), than their almost juridical role: in earlier Greek, ἄνδρες (sometimes preceded by ὦ, the vocative address, "O") is frequent in the familiar address, "*Gentlemen* of the jury" (LSJ, *s.v.* ἀνήρ VI 1 [p. 138a]).

58:5 • *For those who* (τοὺς μέν): The corresponding τοὺς δέ begins in 58:7.

God. ⁹So then, men,ᵃ choose which of the two paths you prefer: the choice is yours to make."

59 (6 *cont.*) When the crowds heard Andrew's speech they were won over by him, or so it appeared, and they did not leave the spot. ²So the most blessed one continued, even longer than he had before—so that those who heard him took it as a sign. ³For three days and nights he addressed them, and no one, no matter how weary, left his side.

⁴On the fourth day, now that they had observed his nobility, the adamance of his thought, the sheer abundance of his words, the value of his exhortation, ⁵the stability of his soul, the prudence of his spirit, the firmness of his mind, and the precision of his reasoning, they were furious with Aegeates and together ran off to the tribunal. ⁶As he sat there they cried out, "What is this judgment of yours, proconsul? You have judged wickedly! ⁷You have made an unjust decision! Your courts are a sacrilege! ⁸What crime did the man commit? What evil has he done?ᵃ The city is in uproar! ⁹You're wronging us all! You're grieving us all! Don't betray the city of the emperor! ¹⁰Grant the Achaeans the just man! Grant us this god-fearing man! ¹¹Don't kill this man possessed by his God! Don't destroy this pious man. ¹²Sure, he has been hanging <there> for four days—but he's still alive! Although he has eaten nothing, he has glutted us with his words. ¹³Bring the man down, and we'll all become philosophers! Untie this prudent one, and all Patras will be law-abiding! Release this really rational one, and all Achaea will receive mercy!"

60 (7) At first Aegeates disregarded the crowd, and gestured for them to leave the tribunal: but they were enraged, and were gaining courage to oppose him in some way. (They numbered about two thousand). ²When the proconsul saw them he became crazed, or

58:9 ᵃCf. 58:4

59:8 ᵃCf. Mk 15:14; Mt 27:23; Lk 23:22

59:4 • *nobility:* γενναῖος, the root meaning of which is "true to one's birth or descent," in this case Andrew's kinship with the divine.
59:9 • *the city of the emperor* (τὴν καίσαρος πόλιν): There is perhaps more than the hint of a threat here, as in John 19:12 ("If you release this man, you are not Caesar's friend").
59:13 • *become philosophers:* φιλοσοφήσομεν, here perhaps in the sense of "leading a well-regulated life," since a revolution appears imminent (see 60:2; LSJ, *s.v.* I.3 [p. 1939b]).

60:1 *two thousand:* AA Ep Ma 1 "20,000."
60:2 *crazed:* HS "When the proconsul saw that they had become rather crazed."

so it seemed—terrified that he might suffer a revolution. ³He got up from the tribunal and went off with them, promising to release blessed Andrew.

⁴They ran ahead to tell the apostle this very fact, <and to tell him> the reason for Aegeates's arrival. ⁵The truth is that the crowd was jubilant because blessed Andrew was about to be untied; so that when the proconsul arrived all the believersª were rejoicing, along with Maximilla.

61 (8) When Andrew heard this, he said, "Oh, the great lethargy of those I have taught! Oh, the sudden fog engulfing us even after <the revelation of> many mysteries! ²Oh, how much we have spoken up to the present, and we haven't convinced even our own! Oh, how much has happened so that we might escape what's earthly!ª ³Oh, what strong statements have been spoken against carnal things, and yet they want more of the same! Oh, how many times I have prayed that I might lift them from these filthy habits, but instead they were encouraged to nothingness! ⁴Why this excessive fondness for the flesh? Why this great complicity with it? Do you again encourage me to be put back among things in flux? ⁵If you understood that I have been set loose from ropes but tied up to myself, you yourselves would have been eager to be loosened from the many and to be tied to the one. ⁶What am I to say? I'm certain that what I'm saying will happen: you yourselves will I tie up with me and, after liberating myself, I will release myself from everything and become united with the one who came into being for all and who exists beyond all.

62 (8 *cont.*) "But now that Aegeates is coming to me, I'll keep quiet and embrace my children. Whatever I must resolve by speaking to him, these things <alone> I will speak. ²Aegeates, why have you come to us again? Why do you who are foreign to us come to us? What do you want to attempt now? What do you want to set about? Whom do you wish to summon? Say something! ³Have you come to untie us because you changed your mind? Even if you really did change your mind, Aegeates, I could never go along with you. ⁴Were

60:5 ª → AAnMt 3:3

61:2 ªCf. 57:11

61:4 • *be put back*, or "be put on ship" (ἀναθῆναι).

61:4 *N E* "How long will you be devoted to the worldly and ephemeral? When will you comprehend things above us and hasten to lay hold of things there? Let me at last be destroyed in the manner you now see."

you to promise all your possessions, I would keep far away from them. Were you to say you yourself were mine, I wouldn't trust you. ⁵Would you untie the one who is tied up, proconsul? Would you untie the one who has fled? Would you untie the one who was liberated? ⁶Would you untie the one recognized by his kindred, the one who received mercy, the one loved by him, the one alien to you, the stranger who appeared so only to you? ⁷I possess the one with whom I will always be. I possess the one with whom I will be a compatriot for countless ages. ⁸It's to him that I'm going. It's to him that I speed on, to the one who made me recognize even you by saying to me: 'Watch out for Aegeates and his gifts. ⁹Don't let that rogue frighten you, and don't let him suppose that he can seize you, for you are mine. ¹⁰He is your enemy. He's a corrupter, a cheat, a destroyer, a slanderer, a boor, a maniac, a busybody, a murderer, an insolent egotist, a flatterer, a magician, terrible, petulant, unmerciful, and decorated on all sides by his material veneer.' ¹¹I recognized you through your turning to me, and that's why I am <now> released from you. ¹²Proconsul, I know very well that you wail and mourn because of what I'm saying to you as I flee to the one beyond you. ¹³Yes, you will weep, beat your breast, gnash your teeth, grieve, despair, lament, anguish, and behave like your relative, the sea, which you now see furiously stirred up by the waves because I'm leaving you all. ¹⁴But the grace which came because of me is delightful, holy, just, true, charming, and articulate, along with all the things by which you seemed to have been adorned through me."

¹⁵When the proconsul heard these things he stood there flabbergasted—stunned, almost. ¹⁶Andrew looked at him again and said, "Aegeates, enemy of us all, now you stand there watching. Do you stand there quiet and calm, unable to do anything you dare? ¹⁷My kindred and I hurry on to things we have to do, leaving you to be what you are and what you fail to understand about yourself."

63 (9) Aegeates again attempted to approach the wood to untie Andrew, because the entire city was in an uproar against him. ²Andrew the apostle shouted out: "Master, do not permit Andrew, the

---

62:10 • *material* or "wooden" (ὑλώδης).

62:13 *anguish:* Arm adds "and abandon your miserable life."
62:13 *leaving you all:* Arm adds "for <the sea> is like you, and like the world."
62:14 *articulate:* Reading λάλον, or possibly

καλόν, "good"; Arm "will with all the goodness of the holy and true divine word."
62:15 *stunned, almost:* N E Cd add "so the entire city was in an uproar for him to release Andrew."

one tied to your wood, to be untied again. ³Jesus, do not give me to the shameless devil, I who am attached to your mystery. ⁴Father, do not let your opponent untie me, I who am hanging on your grace: may that runt no longer humiliate the one who has known your greatness. ⁵But you yourself, Christ, you whom I desired, whom I loved, whom I know, whom I possess, whom I cherish, whose I am—receive me, so that by my departure to you there may be a reunion of my many kindred, those who rest in your majesty."

⁶When he had said these things and further glorified the Lord, he handed over <his> spirit, so that we wept; everyone <there> grieved his departure.

64 (10) After the departure of the blessed apostle, Maximilla, accompanied by Stratocles, completely disregarded those standing around her and came forward. ²She untied the corpse of the blessed one and, having provided it with the necessary attention, buried it at nightfall.

³She separated from Aegeates because of his bestial soul and lawless public life. Thereafter, though he shammed good behavior, she had nothing whatever to do with him. ⁴Choosing instead a holy and quiet life, provided for by the love of Christ, she spent her time happily with her fellow believers.ᵃ ⁵Even though Aegeates often appealed to her and offered her the opportunity to manage his affairs, he was not able to persuade her. ⁶And so, one night, undetected by anyone in his household, he threw himself from a great height and died.

⁷Stratocles, Aegeates's natural brother, would not so much as touch the property Aegeates left. (The wretch had died childless). ⁸He said, "May your possessions go with you, Aegeates! May Jesus be my friend and I his! ⁹Casting from me the entire lot of external and internal evils and entrusting to that one everything I own, I thrust aside everything opposed to him."

65 (11) Here, then, I must make an end of the blessed tales, acts, and mysteries difficult—or should I say, impossible—to express. Let this stroke of the pen end it: ²I will pray first for myself, that

64:4 ᵃ → AAnMt 3:3

64:8 ᵃCf. Ac 8:20

63:6 • *handed over <his> spirit:* παρέδωκεν τὸ πνεῦμα, as in John 19:30.
64:7 • *childless:* But see 36:3, where Aegeates implies that he and Maximilla have had children.

63:4 *N E* "Father, do not let the one stretched out in your likeness be given slack."

63:6 *his spirit: Ma AA Ep* add "with [*AA Ep*: his] thanksgiving."

I heard what was actually said, both the obvious and also the obscure, comprehensible only to the intellect. ³I will pray next for all who are convinced by what was said, that they may have fellowship with each other, as God opens the ears of the listeners, to make comprehensible all his gifts in Christ Jesus our Lord; ⁴to whom, together with the Father, be glory, honor, and power with the all-holy and good and life-giving Spirit, now and always, forever and ever. Amen.

65:1–4 This postscript appears at the end of *HS* and *AA*, with echoes in Arm (where the passage appears in direct discourse as a continuation of Stratocles's speech).

65:4 *with . . . : HS* "let us send up a common doxology to the philanthropic God with his unique son and. . . ."

Augustine, *Contra Felicem* 6

Augustine claims that one of "Leucius's" Acta contained the following. It would appear likely that it belongs to the *Acts of Andrew*, but it cannot be placed in the Acts with precision.

> Pretentious imaginations, sham displays, and constrictions of things perceptible do not issue from one's true nature but from that human essence which demeans itself through seduction.

The Longer Version of Andrew's Speech to the Cross

Martyrium prius, Laudatio, and the Armenian continue Andrew's speech to the cross after the words "why you were fixed there" in AcAndPas 54:3. In many respects the Armenian appears to provide the earlier version, and it is therefore quite possible that some such continuation appeared in the ancient *Acts of Andrew.*

54 ³ᵃ"I study your image for which you stood: I saw mine in you as I etched yours upon me.
    If what I perceive is you existing, I like what I see, what I
        perceive, what I understand from you.
³ᵇWhat is your shape, O cross? What is your crossbeam?
    Where is the center? What is invisible in you? What is
        apparent?
³ᶜTo what extent are you hidden?
    To what extent are you revealed through the cry of your
        companion <the gallows>?
    To what extent do you labor to find those who hear you?

54:3a M "For you have been planted in the world to stabilize the unstable. One of your timbers extends into heaven so that you might symbolize the heavenly word"; similarly L.
54:3b M L "Your crossbeam spreads to the right and left so that you may put to flight the jealous and opposing power and gather the world [L: things scattered abroad] into a unity."

54:3b *Where is the center?* M "Your base has been planted in the earth so that you might unite with things in heaven all that is on the earth and beneath it"; similarly L.
54:3c M "O cross, implement of salvation of the Most High! O cross, trophy of Christ's victory over his enemies! O cross, planted on earth but bearing fruit in heaven!"; similarly L.

3dO name of the cross, entirely filled with <saving> deeds!
  Well done, O cross, who restrained the error of the world!
3eWell done, vision of violence
    that continually and violently treats violence with
      violence!
  Well done, shape of understanding, who shaped the
    shapeless!
3fWell done, unbounded bond that bound up the first one to
    be unbounded!
  Well done, for the tortures of the invisible,
    previously invisible and incomprehensible!
3gWell done, giver of correction, who corrects the one who
    needs no correction!
  Well done, O cross, who put on the Master,
  produced the thief as your fruit,[a]
  called the apostle to repentance,[b]
  and did not disqualify us from being received.

3hSo then, cross, pure, radiant, and full of life and light, receive
me, the one who for so long has been weary. 3iBut how long shall I
say these things without being embraced by the cross, so that in
the cross I may be made to live, and through the cross I may leave
this life in a death like his? 3jApproach, you ministers of my joy

54:3g [a]Cf. Lk 24:43
[b]Cf. Mt 27:3

54:3d Arm "O name of the cross, filled with all things! What a marvel! What should one say to you, alter Andrew? When God, father of our entire nature, Jesus, communicated his thought to ignorant men who were judges without God at that time, they had neither fire nor sword or dungeons nor strangling ropes nor chains nor starvation nor prison nor stoning nor other instruments <of torture>. They learned that he, on whom they dared to lay a hand, would instead consume the cross. Well done, O cross, called 'perfect power'! Well done, intelligent form, born of an intelligent word! They did not know you, but we have recognized you and because of this we have found mercy. You manifest yourself to me; it induces me to speak."
54:3d Or "who held together the revolving vault of the universe!"; Arm "Well done, O cross, who leaped over the distractions of the world!"
54:3g M "Well done, invisible punishment, who punished visibly the essence of polytheistic knowledge and expelled its inventor from humankind!"
54:3g *put on the Master:* L "bore the Master like a bunch of grapes."
produced the thief as your fruit: N "Greetings, O

cross, by means of whom the thief inhabited paradise."
54:3g *from being received:* Arm continues "Bravo to you, Christ, who remains for me deliverance on the cross, who endured that which you did not deserve. Bravo for the insults you endured for humankind before the shameless one, for you shall shame him. Bravo that you did not flee from the one who could not know what he did. With goodness you endured your torturers, since they did not know what they had done [cf. Luke 23:34]. You saved the wretched and did not reject your enemies. By your absence of malice we knew your grace, for you did not become hostile, but when they turned to you, you accepted them. And those who rejoice in you bore witness to your beneficence."
54:3h Arm "But now accept us who renounced this <life>, accept us who suffer, and deliver us, Lord, who have taken refuge in you."
54:3i Arm "But until when shall I say this and not what you showed, O cross? Standing before you, I commend to you those who are listening, for there is no other time for us to approach this vision, O cross."
54:3j *to the suffering:* L "to the wood."

and servants of Aegeates: fulfill the intention of us both, and bind the lamb to the suffering, the mortal to its crafter, the soul to its Savior."

Bodleian ms Copt. f. 103 (P)

This fragment cannot be attributed with certainty to the *Acts of Andrew*. If it does belong to this *Acts,* it is possible, as Prieur suggests (*Acta Andreae,* 24–25), that it forms part of AcAndGE 22 or 29, in both of which the Lord appears to the apostle.

(I. Recto)

¹ . . .] person [. . .] see me in the member which [. . .]

²Then Jesus said to Andrew, "Come near me, Andrew. Your name is 'Fire': Blessed are you among all people."

³Andrew answered and said to the Savior, "Let me speak to you."

⁴Then he said to him, "Speak, Andrew, you strong pillar."

⁵"As God who is your father lives," Andrew answered, (I. Verso) "<I swear> that I left the house of my father and my mother,ᵃ and, as my soul lives, that I have not gone into it again. ⁶I have not looked on the face of my father or my mother, nor have I looked on the faces of my children and my wife; ⁷but daily I was bearing my spiritual cross, following you and not laying it down from morning to night."

⁷Jesus answered and said, "I recognize this, Andrew, [. . . "

⁸(II. Recto) " . . .] my wife and my little children [. . .

⁹(II. Verso) " . . .] one smaller than one of us who bear your name. I have not desired two coatsᵃ for myself, and even this coat that is on me is on me [. . . "

5 ᵃCf. Mk 10:29; Mt 19:29; Lk 18:29

9 ᵃCf. Mk 6:9; Mt 10:10; Lk 3:11; 9:3

3:3 • *Let me speak to you,* or " Give me the means to speak to you."
3:4 • *pillar* (ⲥⲧⲩⲗⲟⲥ = στῦλος) is used of leading apostles in, e.g., Gal 2:9; *1 Clem.* 5: 2. With "fire" (ⲕⲱϩⲧ) in the Lord's previous speech it recalls the biblical "pillar of fire" (see Exod 13:21, 22; 14:24; Num 14:14; Neh 9:12, 19).
3:6 • This sentence is particularly corrupt; this is due in part to the work of a corrector. Even though Barns's reconstruction is plausible and meaningful, the exact sense remains uncertain.
3:7 • *daily:* The verse as a whole recalls Matt 10:37 and Luke 14:27, where it likewise follows a saying about leaving home and family; but "daily" corresponds only to Luke 9:23 (cf. Mark 8:34; Matt 16:24).

BIBLIOGRAPHY

TEXTS AND TRANSLATIONS

Allberry, C. R. C., *A Manichaean Psalm-Book.* Manichaean Manuscripts in the Chester Beatty Collections 2 (Stuttgart: W. Kohlhammer, 1938).

Barns, J., "A Coptic Apocryphal Fragment in the Bodleian Library," *Journal of Theological Studies* new series 11 (1960) 70–76.

Boenig, Robert, *The Acts of Andrew in the Country of the Cannibals: Translations from the Greek, Latin, and Old English* (Garland Library of Medieval Literature B/70; New York: Garland, 1991).

Bonnet, Maximillian, ed., "Acta Andreae cum laudatione contexta et Martyrium Andreae graece: Passio Andreae latine," *Analecta Bollandiana* 11 (1894) 309–78; reprinted as idem, Supplementum codicis apocryphi 2 (Paris: Klincksieck, 1895) 1–44.

———, ed., "Gregorii episcopi turonensis liber de miraculis beati Andreae apostoli," in Bruno Krusch, ed., *Gregorii episcopi turonensis miracula et opera minora* (Monumenta Germaniae historica, Scriptorum rerum Merovingicarum 1/2; Hanover: Hahn, 1885; reprinted 1969).

———, ed., "Passio Andreae," "Ex Actis Andreae," "Martyrium Andreae prius," "Martyrium Andreae alterum," and "Acta Andreae et Matthiae," in Richard Adelbert Lipsius and idem, eds., *Acta Apostolorum Apocrypha* (2 vols. in 3 parts; Leipzig: Mendelssohn, 1898–1901; reprinted Hildesheim: Georg Olms, 1959) 2/1. 1–37, 38–45, 46–57, 58–64, 65–116.

Budge, E. A. W., "The Preaching of Saint Andrew," "The Martyrdoms of Saint Andrew," and "The Acts of Saints Matthias and Saint Andrew," in idem, *The Contending of the Apostles (Maṣḥafa Gadla Ḥawâryât)* (London: Oxford University Press, 1899–1902; English trans. rev., 1935; reprinted Amsterdam: Philo, 1976) 1. 140–55, 184–88, 307–35 (Ethiopic text); 2. 137–53, 181–85, 307–34 (English translation).

DeBryne, D., "Epistula Titi, discipuli Pauli, de dispositione sanctimonii," *Revue bénédictine de critique, d'histoire ed de littérature religieuses* 37 (1925) 47–72.

Dihle, Albrecht, "Neues zur Thomas-Tradition." *Jahrbuch für Antike und Christentum* 6 (1963) 54–70.

Elliott, J. K., "The Acts of Andrew," in idem, *The Apocryphal New Testament: A Collection of Apocryphal Christian Literature in an English Translation* (Oxford: Clarendon, 1993) 231–302.

Announced by the publisher as the successor to the venerable translation of M. R. James (see below). Includes additional bibliography of modern translations and studies.

117

Erbetta, Mario, ed. and trans., "Gli Atti di Andrea" and "Gli Atti di Andrea e Matteo fra gli Antropofagi," in idem, *Gli apocrifi del Nuovo Testamento* (3 vols. in 4 parts; Casale Monferrato: Marietti, 1966–81; and reprinted) 2. 395–449, 493–505.

Goodwin, Charles Wycliffe, *The Anglo-Saxon Legends of St. Andrew and St. Veronica* (Cambridge: Macmillan, 1851).

Hennecke, Edgar, ed., *Neutestamentliche Apokryphen in Verbindung mit Fachgelehrten in deutscher Überlieferung und mit Einleitungen* (Tübingen: Mohr-Siebeck, 1904). The *Acts of Andrew* (intro. by Hennecke, trans. by Georg Schimmelpfeng): 459–73.

In subsequent editions:

2d German ed., 1924 (*Acts of Andrew* trans. by Hennecke): 249–56;

3d German ed., 1959–64 (2 vols.; ed. with Wilhelm Schneemelcher; *Acts of Andrew* trans. by Manfred Hornschuh): 2. 270–97;

English translation of the 3d ed.: Edgar Hennecke and Wilhelm Schneemelcher, eds., R. McL. Wilson, trans. ed., *New Testament Apocrypha* (2 vols.; London: Lutterworth; Philadelphia: Westminster, 1962–65): 390–425;

4th German ed. = a corrected reprint of the 3d ed.;

5th ed., 1987–89 (ed. by Schneemelcher; *Acts of Andrew* transl. by various scholars) 2. 93–137;

English translation of the 5th ed.: Wilhelm Schneemelcher, ed., R. McL. Wilson, trans. ed. (rev. ed.; Cambridge: Clark; Louisville: Westminster/John Knox, 1991): 2. 101–51;

6th German ed. = a corrected reprint of the 5th ed.

James, Montague Rhodes, trans., "The Acts of Andrew" and "Acts of Andrew and Mathias (Matthew)," in idem, *The Apocryphal New Testament: Being the Apocryphal Gospels, Acts, Epistles, and Apocalypses* (Oxford: Clarendon, 1924; corrected and augmented ed. 1953) 337–63, 453–58.

For half a century this was the standard English translation.

Leloir, Louis, ed. and trans., *Écrits apocryphes sur les apôtres: Traduction de l'édition arménienne de Venise*, vol. 1: *Pierre, Paul, André, Jacques, Jean* (Corpus Scriptorum Series Apocryphorum 3; Turnhout: Brepols, 1986).

Lipsius, Richard Adelbert and Maximillian Bonnet, eds., *Acta Apostolorum Apocrypha* (2 vols. in 3 parts; Leipzig: Mendelssohn, 1898–1901; reprinted Hildesheim: Georg Olms, 1959).

MacDonald, Dennis Ronald, ed. and trans., *The Acts of Andrew and the Acts of Andrew and Matthias in the City of the Cannibals* (Society of Biblical Literature Texts and Translations 33; Christian Apocrypha 1; Atlanta: Scholars Press, 1990).

Moraldi, Luigi, ed. and trans., "Atti di Andrea," in idem, *Apocrifi del Nuovo Testamento* (2 vols.; Classici delle religioni 5: Le altre confessione critiane; Turin: Piemme, 1971; and reprinted) 2. 429–507.

Piñero, Antonio, and Gonzalo del Cerro, eds. and trans., "Hechos de Andrés," in idem, *Hechos apócrifos de los Apóstoles 1: Hechos de Andrés, Juan y Pedro* (Biblioteca de autores cristianos 646; Madrid: Biblioteca de Autores Cristianos, 2004) 109–235.

Quispel, Gilles, "An Unknown Fragment of the Acts of Andrew (Pap. Copt. Utrecht N.1)," *Vigiliae Christianae* 10 (1956) 129–48 and plate; reprinted in idem, *Gnostic Studies* (2 vols.; Uitgaven van het Nederlands historisch-archaeologisch Instituut te Istanbul 34; Istanbul: Nederlands Historisch-Archaeologisch Instituut in het Nabije Oosten, 1974–1975) 2. 271–87.

Prieur, Jean-Marc, ed. and trans., *Acta Andreae* (Corpus Christianorum Series Apocryphorum 5–6; Turnhout: Brepols, 1989).

————, trans., *Actes de l'apôtre André: Présentation et traduction du latin, du copte et du grec* (Apocryphes: Collection de Poche de L'AELAC 7; Turnhout: Brepols, 1995).

Wright, William, ed. and trans., "The History of Mār Matthew and Mār Andrew, the Blessed Apostles," in idem, *Apocryphal Acts of the Apostles Edited from Syrian Manuscripts in the British Museum and Other Libraries* (London: Williams & Norgate, 1871; reprinted Amsterdam: Philo, 1968) 1. 102–26 (Syriac text); 2. 93–115 (English translation).

STUDIES

Baker, Alfred T., "The Passion of Saint Andrew," *Modern Language Review* 11 (1916) 420–29.

Baumler, Ellen B., "Andrew in the City of the Cannibals: A Comparative Study of the Latin, Greek, and Old English Texts" (Ph.D. diss., University of Kansas, 1985).

Blatt, Franz, *Die lateinischen Bearbeitungen der Acta Andreae et Matthiae apud Anthrophagos* (Beihefte zur Zeitschrift für die neutestamentliche Wissenschaft 12; Giessen: Töpelmann, 1930).

Boenig, Robert, *Saint and Hero: "Andreas" and Medieval Doctrine*. (Lewisburg: Bucknell University Press, 1991).

Bonnet, Maximillian, "La Passion de l'apôtre André en quelle langue a-t-elle été écrite?" *Byzantinische Zeitschrift* 3 (1894) 458–69.

Bovon, François, ed., *Les Actes apocryphes des apôtres: Christianisme et monde païen* (Publications de la Faculté de Théologie de l'Université de Genève 4; Geneva: Labor et Fides, 1981).

————, Ann Graham Brock, and Christopher R. Matthews, eds., *The Apocryphal Acts of the Apostles: Harvard Divinity School Studies* (Religions of the World; Cambridge, Mass.: Harvard University Press / Harvard University Center for the Study of World Religions, 1999).

Bremmer, Jan N., ed., *The Apocryphal Acts of Andrew* (Studies on the Apocryphal Acts of the Apostles 5; Louvain: Peeters, 2000).

Thirteen essays and extensive bibliography.

Brooks, Kenneth R., *Andreas and the Fates of the Apostles* (Oxford: Oxford University Press, 1961).

Burrus, Virginia, *Chastity as Autonomy: Women in the Stories of Apocryphal Acts* (Studies in Women and Religion 23; Lewiston: Edwin Mellen, 1987).

Davies, Stevan L., *The Revolt of the Widows: The Social World of the Apocryphal Acts* (Carbondale: Southern Illinois University Press, 1980).

Detorakis, Theodor, "Τὸ ἀνέκδοτο μαρτύριο τοῦ ἀποστόλου Ἀνδρέα," *Acts of the Second International Congress of Peloponnesian Studies* (Athens: Hetairia Peloponnesiakon Spondon, 1981–1982) 2. 325–52.

Dvornik, F., *The Idea of Apostolicity in Byzantium and the Legend of the Apostle Andrew* (Dumbarton Oaks Studies 4; Cambridge, Mass.: Harvard University Press, 1958).

Flamion, J., *Les Actes apocryphes de l'Apôtre André: Les Actes d'André et de Matthias, de Pierre et de'André et les textes apparentés* (Recueil de travaux d'histoire et de philologie 33; Louvain: Bureaux de Recueil / Paris: Picard / Brussels: Dewit, 1911).

Gil, Juan, "Sobre el texto de los Acta Andreae et Matthiae apud anthropophagos," *Habis* 6 (1975) 177–94.

Gutschmid, Alfred von, "Die Königsnamen in den apokryphen Apostelgeschichten: Ein Beitrag zur Kenntnis des geschichtlichen Romans," *Rheinisches Museum für Philologie* neue Folge 19 (1864) 161–83, 380–401; reprinted in idem, *Kleine Schriften* (5 vols.; Leipzig: Teubner, 1890).

Hennecke, Edgar, and Georg Schimmelpfeng, "Andreasakten," in Hennecke, ed., *Handbuch zu den Neutestamentlichen Apokryphen* (Tübingen: Mohr-Siebeck, 1904) 544–62.
Detailed notes on text and translation. Published as a companion to the first ed. of Hennecke, *Neutestamentliche Apokryphen* (see above).

Junod, Eric, "Créations romanesques et traditions ecclésiastiques dans les Actes apocryphes des apôtres: L'Alternative Fiction romanesque — vérité historique: une impasse," *Augustinianum* 23 (1983) 271–85.

Krapp, George Philip, *Andreas and the Fates of the Apostles: Two Anglo-Saxon Narrative Poems* (Boston / New York: Ginn, 1906).

Lemm, Oskar von, "Koptische apokryphe Apostelakten," *Mélanges asiatiques tirés du Bulletin Impériale des Sciences de Saint Pétersbourg* 10 (1890) 99–171.

Lipsius, Richard Adelbert, *Die apokryphen Apostelgeschichten und Apostellegenden* (3 vols.; Braunschweig: C. A. Schwetschke, 1883–1890; and reprinted).

Löfstedt, Bengt, "Zu den lateinischen Bearbeitungen der Acta Andreae et Matthiae apud Anthropophagos," *Habis* 6 (1975) 167–76.

MacDonald, Dennis Ronald, "*The Acts of Andrew and Matthias* and *The Acts of Andrew*," and "Response," in idem, ed., *The Apocryphal Acts of Apostles = Semeia* 38 (1986) 9–26, 35–39.

———, *Christianizing Homer: The Odyssey, Plato, and The Acts of Andrew* (New York / Oxford: Oxford University Press, 1994).

Morris, R., *The Blickling Homilies of the Tenth Century* (Early English Text Society 63; London: Trübner, 1880).

Peterson, Peter Megill, *Andrew, Brother of Simon Peter: His History and Legends* (Novum Testamentum Supplements 1; Leiden: E. J. Brill, 1958; reprinted 1963).

Prieur, Jean-Marc, "Les Actes apocryphes de l'apôtre André: Présentation des diverses traditions apocryphes et état de la question," *Aufstieg und Niedergang der römischen Welt* 2.25.6 (1988) 4383–4414.

Reinach, Salomon, "Les apôtres chez les anthropophages," *Revue d'histoire et de littérature religieuse* 9 (1904) 305–20.

Root, Robert Kilburn, *Andreas: The Legend of St. Andrew* (Yale Studies in English 7; New York: Henry Holt, 1899).

Söder, Rosa, *Die apokryphen Apostelgeschichten und die romanhafte Literatur der Antike* (Würzburger Studien zur Altertumswissenschaft 3; Stuttgart: Kohlhammer, 1932; reprinted Darmstadt: Wissenschaftliche Buchgesellschaft, 1969).

INDEX

OLD TESTAMENT

The Index has been compiled by Robert Foster

JEWISH APOCRYPHA
AND PSEUDEPIGRAPHA

NEW TESTAMENT

CHRISTIAN APOCRYPHA

OTHER EARLY
CHRISTIAN LITERATURE

OTHER ANCIENT WRITINGS